PRAISE FOR OTHER BOOKS BY
KEN WHITING AND ALEX MATTHEWS

"The sheer joy and sharp technique in your books and videos
has everything to do with both our progress in learning and
our happiness in achieving."
George Baldwin

"Thanks for creating such excellent instruction on kayaking."
Gary Bodnar

"A fantastic complement to any kayaker's library."
Eugene Buchanan, Editor, Paddler Magazine

"The Heliconia Press is clearly committed to producing
the most detailed, concise and entertaining instructional
products on the market."
Richard Parkin, Editor, Paddles Magazine

"Terrific instruction!"
Philippe Doux, Editor, Kayak Session/Paddle World Magazine

ALSO AVAILABLE

Canoeing The Essential Skills & Safety
$19.95

Sea Kayaking Rough Waters
$19.95

Winter Backpacking
$19.95

Ice Fishing: The Ultimate Guide
$24.95

Kayak Fishing: The Ultimate Guide 2nd Edition
$24.95

Kayak Bass Fishing
$24.95

Recreational Kayaking The Ultimate Guide
$19.95

Whitewater Kayaking The Ultimate Guide—2nd Edition
$26.95

Kayaking for Fitness
$19.95

Camp Cooking in the Wild
$19.95

Rolling a Kayak
$16.95

Canoe Camping
$16.95

Outdoor Parents, Outdoor Kids
$19.95

Torrent
$29.95

The Playboater's Handbook II
$22.95

Kayak Fishing: Game On 2 DVD
$24.95

Filleting Fish—Freshwater DVD
$12.95

Running The Essential Guide DVD
$19.95

Knots to Know DVD
$14.96

Whitewater Kayaking—DVD Box Set
$49.95

Kayak Fishing: Game On DVD
$24.95

Kayak Fishing The Ultimate Guide DVD
$19.95
Canoeing **with Andrew Westwood DVD**
$19.95

Rolling a Kayak—Whitewater DVD
$26.95

Rolling a Kayak—Sea Kayak DVD
$26.95

Recreational Kayaking The Essential Skills and Safety DVD
$19.95

Recreational Kayaking for Women DVD
$24.95

b.EAST DVD
$19.95

Sea Kayaking: The Ultimate Guide DVD
$29.95

Whitewater Kayaking with Ken Whiting DVD
$29.95

Playboating with Ken Whiting DVD
$29.95

The Paddling Chef, Second Edition
$16.95

TOURING & SEA
KAYAKING
The Essential Skills and Safety

Alex Matthews and Ken Whiting

THE **HELICONIA PRESS**

an Imprint of Fox Chapel Publishing
www.FoxChapelPublishing.com

Photography by: Paul Villecourt, except as noted.
Illustrations by: Paul Mason
Design & Layout: Robyn Hader
Editor: Rebecca Sandiford

ISBN 978-1-896980-71-3

Library of Congress Cataloging-in-Publication Data

Matthews, Alex, 1964-

Touring & sea kayaking / by Alex Matthews and Ken Whiting.

    p. cm.

Includes index.

Originally published: Ontario : Heliconia Press, 2006.

ISBN 978-1-896980-71-3

1. Kayak touring. 2. Sea kayaking. I. Whiting, Ken. II. Title.

GV789.M38 2012

797.1224--dc23

                    2011051643

To learn more about the other great books from Fox Chapel Publishing, or to find a retailer near you, call toll-free 800-457-9112 or visit us at *www.FoxChapelPublishing.com*.

Note to Authors: We are always looking for talented authors to write new books. Please send a brief letter describing your idea to Acquisition Editor, 1970 Broad Street, East Petersburg, PA 17520.

Printed in China
First printing

TABLE OF CONTENTS

ACKNOWLEDGEMENTS

When the book is finally in our hands, we will assuredly reflect on the journey that was required for its completion. These thoughts will without a doubt revolve around the many people who lent their support and made the book possible. First and foremost, we thank our wives, Rochelle and Nicole, who continue to show great patience and understanding in regards to our obsession with kayaks.

Special thanks go to everyone else who was part of getting here.

In Maine, we thank Peggy and Michael of Mermaid's Purse Farm for opening their home to us, and Bill Zoelich for sharing his coastline.

In Saint John, New Brunswick, we thank Harold Cox, Wendy Hughes of Go Fundy Events, and Sally Cummings of Tourism Saint John.

In Cape Breton, Nova Scotia, we send our thanks to Debbie Martell of the Cape Breton Highlands Project, Jill Humphries of the Ingonish Chalets, Mike Crimp of Cape Breton Sea Coast Adventures, Angelo Spinazzola of North River Kayak Tours, and Mike Fitzgerald and Jennifer Moses of Eagle North Canoe and Kayak.

We'd also like to send our sincere thanks to our friends who have provided ongoing support to our projects and who played a significant role in making this book a reality. Thanks go to Nando Zucchi and Sara Knies of Necky Kayaks, Chris Jacobs of Extrasport, Craig Langford and Joe Matuska of Aquabound, Morgan Goldie of North Water, Rich Wilson of Snap Dragon, Lisa Beckstead, Marta Miller and Michael Duffy of Kokatat, and Mike May of Brunton.

Finally, thanks go to Paul Villecourt for putting up with all our dumb jokes and for always getting the shot; to Robyn Hader, Paul Mason, Rebecca Sandiford, Lisa Utronki, Ruth Gordon, and the rest of the The Heliconia Press crew.

INTRODUCTION

Kayaking is one of the most approachable outdoor sports around and has something to offer everyone. For some, kayaking simply represents a favorite way to get fresh air and exercise while leaving the stress and concerns of everyday life behind. Others look to kayaking as an enjoyable way to explore and experience the outdoors recreationally. The more audacious will use kayaks as a tool for exploration and adventure. Whatever your end goal might be, as long as you are reasonably fit and enjoy being on the water, then kayaking is for you.

Although there are many different forms of kayaking, this book focuses on sea kayaking, which is also known as kayak touring when done on inland waterways. Sea kayaks are the luxury sedans of the kayak world, specifically designed to allow the most efficient and comfortable travel possible over extended distances. In fact, as many intrepid expedition paddlers have proven, there is almost no limit to where a kayak can take you. Local rivers, lakes, and ponds provide some great kayaking, while those fortunate enough to live close to the sea enjoy access to a different and dramatic paddling experience. Wherever you paddle, be assured that after hopping

into a kayak for the first time, you'll enjoy a new perspective and appreciation for the marine environment, in all its beauty and diversity.

This book is designed to provide new or interested kayakers with the skills and knowledge necessary to get into the sport of kayaking comfortably and safely. More experienced paddlers will also find advanced techniques and drills to help hone their skills. With this in mind, it must be understood that nothing can replace the value of professional "live" instruction, and we would strongly urge you to take a course through an established school or paddling club. Not only will you get to practice skills on the water and get valuable feedback; these forums also provide the best means of meeting other paddlers with similar interests. Many outfitters and touring companies also offer a variety of guided trips suitable for beginner paddlers. For many, this can offer a terrific introduction to kayaking and be a great means of testing the waters to see if the sport is something that you want to pursue.

If you already paddle, then I hope this book helps you progress, and that it provides a stepping-stone that allows you to reach your goals. If you're new to kayaking, then let me take this opportunity to congratulate you for taking the first steps towards being one of the remarkably few people in this world who will experience the wonders of sea kayaking. I'm sure you'll find that on the days that you paddle, the rest of your world seems a little brighter.

ABOUT THE AUTHORS

ALEX MATTHEWS

Alex Matthews is a whitewater paddler, kayak-surfer and passionate sea kayaker. He has guided sea kayak trips in many areas around Vancouver Island, the Queen Charlotte Islands, and Baja, Mexico. He has explored sections of both the West and East Coasts of Canada and the United States. A successful writer known for his irreverent wit and humor, his articles have appeared in many prominent paddlesports publications, and he has worked in both kayak design and marketing for prominent paddlesport companies.

His abiding fascination for any liquid environment in general and the ocean in particular fuels his zeal for crafts that interact with water as directly as possible. It is no surprise that his Zodiac sign is Pisces—the fish.

KEN WHITING

After winning the World Freestyle Kayaking Championships in 1997, Ken focused his passion for paddling on the development of instructional tools. Ken is now one of the most influential paddlers in the world, and was recognized as such by Paddler Magazine as one of their "Paddlers of the Century." He has paddled on over 200 rivers in 15 countries and has ten best-selling, award-winning instructional books and DVDs to his name. Ken and his wife Nicole live in Beachburg, Canada, where they run The Heliconia Press. For more information, visit www.helipress.com

CHAPTER ONE

EQUIPMENT

BODY • THE KAYAK • THE PADDLE • PERSONAL GEAR

BODY

When we consider paddling equipment, it's all too easy to forget about our own bodies. But, without a doubt, your body is your most important piece of equipment. It is the engine that will power your kayak forward, so it's key to keep that motor running smoothly. It should go without saying that warming up and stretching before and after paddling is a good idea. While it's obvious to stretch the arms and upper body, don't forget about your lower body either. In particular, tight hamstrings can make the sitting position in a kayak uncomfortable.

Most injuries in kayaking are minor ones, stemming from overuse. Wrist issues like carpal tunnel or tendonitis are common, as are sore backs or shoulders. To avoid these injuries, start slowly and listen to what your body is telling you. Understand that kayaking will use your muscles in new ways, and that it will take time to build your paddling strength and stamina. Although sea kayaking can be an incredibly low impact sport and you don't need to be in great shape to do it, the reality is that the stronger and more flexible that you become, the more comfortable and confident you can be in your boat.

When it comes to stretching, the legs are often forgotten, but tight hamstrings will make the sitting position in a kayak uncomfortable.

THE KAYAK

Originating in Canada's North and Greenland, kayaks were traditionally made from sealskin stretched over a wooden frame. This approach is still popular with some kayakers today, who use more durable modern fabrics instead of sealskin. While most commercially available kayaks are now built from a plastic called polyethylene, or composite materials like fiberglass, Kevlar or Carbon, the traditional kayaks are honored in every design produced today.

Polyethylene kayaks are very affordable, and have amazing durability. Nothing beats a poly boat when it comes to absorbing big impacts or standing up to serious abuse. Poly kayaks will tend to deform over time, especially when exposed to heat (like really hot sun), but require minimal maintenance. For these reasons, poly kayaks are the best choice for rental operations or play sessions around rocks, where collisions with immovable objects are likely.

Composite boats are stiffer, lighter and shinier than plastic ones. They are also about twice the price! Kevlar and Carbon kayaks are slightly lighter (5-8 lbs) than fiberglass ones, but are even more expensive. In my experience, Kevlar and Carbon are not worth the extra expense unless weight is really a key concern. The minor weight savings of a few pounds will only be noticeable when carrying the kayak and won't be detectable when afloat. Composite kayaks feel sweeter in the water than poly boats, and seem to exhibit more glide. While they are subject to more damage from heavy collisions than polymer kayaks, composites will lasts for years if treated carefully, and are actually far more durable than most people suspect. I have had the best durability from fiberglass models in the 55 lbs and above range.

The latest development in kayak construction involves a manufacturing process called thermoforming. This process uses a vacuum to draw heated plastic sheet material (acrylic-capped ABS) over a mold to create parts. Thermoformed kayaks provide a good compromise between the durability and affordability of polyethylene boats and the beauty and lightness of composite ones.

Another type of boat that you may see on the water is the folding kayak. Folding kayaks are constructed with a collapsible, folding frame covered by a high-tech fabric skin, which can all be broken down and packed away in a large backpack. This makes them an ideal boat for air travel and long-term storage.

ANATOMY

The top of a kayak is referred to as the deck, and the bottom is the hull. The front is called the bow, and the back end is the stern. The cockpit is the opening in the deck where you sit, and the coaming is the lip of the cockpit where the spray deck attaches to the kayak.

On the deck, you'll find an array of bungee cords for storing chart cases, extra gear and a spare paddle. Many boats are also equipped with perimeter lines that make grabbing the kayak easier, which is a big asset when performing rescues.

The interior volume of a kayak should be divided into three or more waterproof compartments. The dividing walls are called bulkheads. The central compartment is where you sit, and is accessed through the cockpit. The other compartments are accessed through hatches. These compartments aren't only great for storing cargo; they're also a key safety feature for a sea kayak. When sealed, they provide the essential flotation that prevents a boat from sinking if it capsizes. There is a variety of closure systems used for hatches, from neoprene gaskets combined with rigid shells, to one-piece rubber hatch covers. Each system has its own merits and limitations.

Most kayaks have a skeg or a rudder, both of which are designed to help keep a boat running straight. Rudders are deployed from their stored position by use of haul lines found alongside the cockpit. Likewise, skegs are usually controlled by a slider located on deck by the paddler's knee. Rudders are controlled by foot-pedals in the boat, and swing from side to side. Skegs do not pivot side to side like rudders, but simply lower straight into the water. How deeply the skeg is deployed (controlled by the slider)

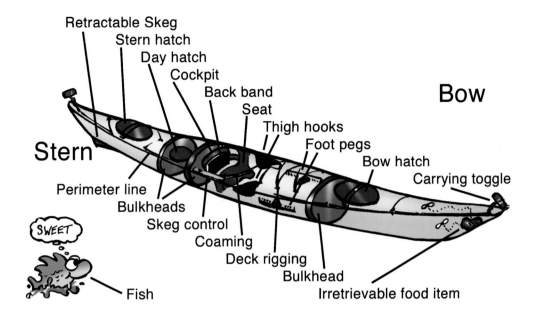

Retractable Skeg
Stern hatch
Day hatch
Cockpit
Back band
Seat
Thigh hooks
Foot pegs
Bow hatch
Carrying toggle
Bow
Stern
Perimeter line
Bulkheads
Skeg control
Coaming
Deck rigging
Bulkhead
Irretrievable food item
SWEET
Fish

dictates how much the skeg affects the kayak's direction.

There are pros and cons to both skegs and rudders. Skegs are tucked up out of the way when not in use, and less prone to damage than rudders; but rudders provide the most control. Either way, it's important that you understand that rudders and skegs are not substitutes for good paddling skills. In this book, we will demonstrate all strokes without the use of rudders or skegs, because kayaks are primarily controlled by paddle strokes, edging (tilting the boat toward one side) and good technique.

Inside the cockpit, you'll find various pieces of outfitting that are designed to provide comfort and control over your kayak. A contoured seat makes sitting more comfortable and helps keep your butt in place. A back band will support your lower back and promote good posture. Thigh hooks wrap around the thighs and provide the real control over a kayak's edging. Foot pedals adjust to accommodate paddlers with different leg lengths, and, for kayaks equipped with rudders, slide fore and aft to control the rudder's movement side-to-side.

BOAT DESIGN AND SELECTION

The days of 'one-size-fits-all' kayaks are gone. Boat design is now a sophisticated process performed by professional designers, involving prototype testing and flashy software packages that provide digital simulations. These advances in boat design ensure that there is a kayak out there built for someone just like you.

Rocker

Rocker refers to the curvature of the hull from bow to stern, as viewed from the side. The more rocker a boat has, the more easily it will turn, but the less effectively it will hold a line, or 'track'. The rocker in the last three feet of the stern has an especially large impact on how easily a kayak will turn or how well it will track.

Volume

The volume of a kayak refers to the air space inside the boat. High-volume kayaks are great for carrying equipment and are great for camping trips. The downside of high-volume kayaks is that they invariably sit high above the water, which makes them a lot more susceptible to being pushed around by wind and waves.

Length

The length of a kayak will have an impact on a number of performance issues. In general, longer kayaks are faster, have more carrying capacity and track (go straight) more easily than shorter kayaks. Shorter kayaks are generally more maneuverable on the water and are lighter and easier to transport.

Width

The beam of a kayak (its width as viewed from above) has the biggest effect on how stable it is on the water. In general, the wider a kayak is, the more stable it will feel. The narrower a kayak is, the less stable it will be, but the faster it will travel through the water.

Hull Shapes

Flat Hull:

Flat hulls make for the most stable kayaks on calm flat water. The downside of flat hulls is that they are the most difficult to hold on edge and do not perform very well in waves.

Rounded Hull:

A rounded hull makes for a fast kayak that performs well in virtually all conditions and can be held on its edges most easily. The downside of the rounded hull is that it isn't as stable in calm flat water.

V-Shaped Hull:

A V-shaped hull provides a good compromise between a round and flat hull. V-shaped hulls perform well in most conditions, are easily held on edge, and are quite stable.

The three main hull shapes: flat, rounded, and V-shaped.

CHOOSING A KAYAK

If you're shopping for a kayak, the most important thing to do is to identify the type of paddling that you're interested in and will be spending most of your time doing. With the help of someone knowledgeable, you can then narrow down your options considerably. Your final decision should be made based on the following factors: your size and weight, your comfort level in the boat, your budget, and any other personal preferences such as hatch systems, seat comfort, or overall aesthetics.

Regardless of how much research and self-evaluation you do, before you buy a kayak, make sure that you take the time to get it on the water for a test drive.

THE PADDLE

If you are the motor for your kayak, then the paddle is the drive shaft that allows you to propel the boat forward. Paddles have three main parts: a shaft, a power face, and a back face. The power face is the side of the paddle that catches water when you take a forward stroke.

Paddles are most commonly made from plastic, fiberglass, carbon fiber, or wood. Plastic blades offer a great blend of performance and affordability, while fiberglass is lighter and stiffer, but costs significantly more. Carbon fiber yields the lightest weights and tremendous stiffness, but costs even more than fiberglass. A stiff paddle provides additional power for each of your strokes, but may also be more jarring to your joints

21

because the paddle absorbs less shock. Wood has a nice 'warm' feel, and is favored by kayakers who prefer the long, narrow, quill shape of traditional Greenland paddles.

When choosing a paddle, the two most important factors that you'll need to consider are its length and its blade size. The type of paddling that you do, and your physical size will play the largest roles in your decision making process.

The most common length for sea kayaking paddles is between 210 and 230 cm. Generally, a smaller paddler should use smaller blades and a shorter shaft, while a stronger paddle can control a paddle with larger blades and a longer shaft.

As we just mentioned though, the type of paddling that you plan to do should play an equally important role in your paddle decision. Shorter paddles promote a paddle stroke that is closer to vertical, which suits a more active paddling style; longer paddles facilitate a lower angle stroke, which is preferable for covering longer distances.

As for the size of your blades, long, skinny blades, with fairly small surface areas, are preferred for long distance paddling. These paddles will often

Shorter paddles with larger blades suit more active paddlers. Longer paddles with narrower blades are preferable for more relaxed paddling or when covering longer distances.

have a soft dihedral shape to their power face, which means the two faces of the blade on either side of the center line slope away slightly. This causes the paddle to 'catch' less water, which allows for a smoother and less energy-consuming stroke. For more active paddling, which uses more vertical strokes, a wider, more 'squarish' blade, with more of a 'cup' shape is preferred, because it catches more water and provides more power with each stroke. Racing paddles, otherwise known as wing paddles, take this to the extreme, with an ultra-aggressive power face designed to catch a maximum amount of water.

Once you've decided on a paddle length and blade size, you'll need to make a few other decisions, the largest being the 'feather', or offset of your blades. Feather is the amount of twist between the blades of a paddle. One nice thing is that most touring paddles come as two-piece designs that provide multiple feather options. A 60-degree offset is most common, although some kayakers prefer a higher offset, and others will use a flat or zero-degree feather. The advantage of feathering the blade is that in a headwind the top blade slices through the air and offers much less resistance. On the other hand, a lower offset is more intuitive and means less repetitive twisting of your wrist, which can help prevent tendonitis. There is no 'right way' here, just personal preference. One thing that I would recommend is that once you decide on a degree of feather for yourself, do not change it. When you're reacting to things happening to your kayak, you need to know immediately and instinctively how your blades are going to contact the water.

Something else you might see on the water are paddles with bent shafts. The goal of bent shaft paddles is to lessen wrist and muscle fatigue by placing the joints of the hand and wrist in a more natural position when taking a stroke. Because of the added complexity of manufacturing the shaft, these paddles are often quite costly. There's endless debate on how effective bent shafts really are – try one yourself and make up your own mind!

A feathered paddle, with blades offset from each other, is less intuitive to use, but in a headwind the top blade slices through the air and offers much less resistance. 23

In reality, you'll actually need two paddles, because a spare should be carried on deck in case you suddenly can't use your primary paddle due to damage or loss. The backup need not be exactly the same model, but it should be more than good enough to provide a competent replacement for your primary paddle.

TIP

It's a good idea to use a paddle with brightly-colored blades. From a safety perspective, it will make you more visible on the water, and will make the paddle more useful as a way to catch attention in case of emergency. A bright paddle will also lower the chances of it being lost. Even in calm conditions, a dark paddle can be incredibly hard to spot from water level. If you have a dark colored paddle, you can use stickers or reflective tape to increase its visibility.

PERSONAL GEAR

Having the right gear on the water, and in camp, will make a huge difference to your level of enjoyment, so while it makes sense to shop for a good bargain, don't scrimp too much, and be sure to buy good quality gear. It will keep you drier, warmer, safer, more comfortable, more confident, and allow you to have more fun on the water.

PFD

Your life jacket or 'personal flotation device' (PFD) is the most important piece of safety equipment, so make sure that you take the time to find one that is Coast Guard approved and that is comfortable enough that you won't ever feel the need to take it off while on the water. Kayaking-specific models are by far the best because they deliver the flotation you need, in low-profile designs that don't restrict movement.

A proper-fitting PFD should be very snug, but still comfortable when cinched down. A quick and easy test on dry land is to haul up on the shoulder straps to make sure that the jacket stays in place and doesn't ride up around your ears.

There are a lot of good-looking PFDs to choose from, but when it comes to safety it's best to choose a vest in a bright color that can be easily seen from a distance. Many

Kayaking specific PFDs offer large arm holes and minimal material around the shoulders so as not to restrict movement.

lifejackets have reflective tape on them, which makes them even more visible at night or in failing light. Other features might include pockets and built-in tow systems. Pockets are great for stashing items that you'll want to have readily available, like energy bars, whistles, and sunscreen lotion. Tow systems can also come in handy, although it's a good idea to be trained in their use before donning one. Some PFDs also feature pouches for hydration bladders—an excellent option that makes drinking while afloat incredibly convenient.

SPRAY SKIRT

The spray skirt, or spray deck, is responsible for sealing off the cockpit of your kayak and keeping water out of your boat as you paddle. Spray skirts are generally made out of either nylon or neoprene. Nylon decks vent better, which makes them great for paddling in warm conditions, and they also cost less. The downside to nylon decks is that they don't keep water out as well as neoprene skirts do. To provide the best of both worlds, you'll find skirts that mix the materials, having a neoprene deck for dryness and a nylon tunnel for comfort.

Some skirts mix materials, having a neoprene deck for dryness and a nylon tunnel for comfort.

Cockpits of kayaks are not uniform in size, so you'll need to find a skirt that fits your particular boat. There are skirts with adjustable shock cords that can be used on any kayak. These adjustable skirts are a good, economical option for paddlers who will be staying in sheltered waters, but they don't offer a great seal. If you will be dealing with any type of surf, wind, waves, or current, the best skirts are specifically sized to a particular boat's coaming. These skirts will have a rubber rand or perimeter-sewn bungee that may be a little harder to get on, but will keep you much drier. Skirts of this kind generally have two sizes associated with them—the tube (waist) size, and the cockpit size, which refers to the kayak that it is designed to fit. Most manufacturers have a 'fit list' that specifies what skirt/cockpit size is best for each kayak model.

All spray skirts have ripcords for pulling the skirt off the boat when you need to get out. Always make sure that the ripcord is out when you put on the skirt—it is easy to tuck it under the skirt by accident. It's extremely important that you can reliably pop the skirt off the coaming by pulling on the ripcord. If you can't, choose a looser fitting skirt.

DRY BAGS

Although the storage compartments of touring and sea kayaks are considered waterproof, make no mistake—dry bags are the only way to keep your stuff completely dry. The most common dry bags use a roll-top closure and are available in a wide range of sizes, but anything over 20 liters in volume is going to be very difficult to get through the hatches of the average single kayak. The most appropriate dry bag sizes for kayaks are 5, 10, and 20 liters.

*In warm conditions, a short sleeved paddling jacket and/or
a rash guard is a good option.*

DRESSING FOR WARM CONDITIONS

For those of you lucky enough to be dressing for warm conditions, your biggest challenge will be to stay cool and protected from the sun—even on overcast days. The best and easiest defense against the sun is to wear a hat and sunglasses and to use sunscreen. With regards to clothing, it's a good idea to cover as much exposed skin as possible with a light layer. Some fabrics are even treated to protect you from the sun and actually carry an SPF rating. To stay cool in your kayak, quick-drying shorts and sandals work well.

Even in warm conditions, it's usually a good idea to bring a slightly warmer option, especially if you've got a big day planned. Things can cool down very quickly if the wind picks up and dark clouds roll in.

DRESSING FOR COLD CONDITIONS

Picking out what to wear when paddling in cold water can be tricky, especially when the air is warm. Your clothing needs to be comfortable to paddle in, and yet warm enough to protect you if you capsize and find yourself in the water for an extended period of time. The key is to use multiple layers of fabrics that deal with moisture well and dry quickly. The great thing about layering is that it allows you to fine-tune your clothing system and control your body temperature throughout the day.

Under Layers

For your lower body, a farmer john wetsuit is good, affordable insurance against the cold, especially if there's a decent chance that you'll be getting wet. If you are confident that you'll be staying dry, you can wear thermal underwear and fleece under a paddling pant as a more comfortable option.

For your upper body, thermal underwear provides an ideal base layer as it wicks moisture away from your body. Depending on the conditions, you may need a few layers of thermal underwear. On the coldest days, you may even want to wear a fleece overtop.

Cotton is one of the all-time worst materials to wear around cold water. Not only is it very slow to dry (think about how your cotton jeans are always the last thing to be done in the dryer), but it generates a tremendous amount of convective cooling. This means that it actually draws heat out of your body.

Outer Layers

For your lower body, a wetsuit will usually provide enough insulation, especially since your feet and legs will be well-protected from the elements by your kayak. For additional warmth though, paddling pants are recommended. Paddling pants provide protection from the wind and help retain body heat if you're standing around on shore.

A farmer john wetsuit is good, affordable insurance against the cold and wetness.

Thermal underwear provides an ideal base and can be layered comfortably and effectively.

When in a kayak, you are most exposed to the elements above the waist, so you'll want some type of paddling top to protect you from wind and water. A dry top with latex seals or gaskets at the neck and wrists will keep water out, but may be too warm in some conditions. Paddling tops without latex gaskets won't keep the water out in the case of a swim, but depending on the conditions, they can be a good compromise between your concern about cold water immersion, and your comfort level while dry and paddling. Although pricier, waterproof breathable fabrics like Gore-Tex are more comfortable because they breathe better than coated nylon fabrics do, and allow some sweat vapor to escape through the garment. In calm, cool conditions, I like to use a top that only has latex gaskets on the wrists. It's more comfortable around the neck, but it keeps those cold, evil splashes of water from running up the sleeve and down your sides. When the weather is miserable, a hood is also a great addition to a paddling top.

When immersion in cold water is likely, the ultimate defense is a Gore-Tex drysuit. These garments are incredibly comfortable and, when combined with insulating undergarments, provide amazing protection from cold water.

An anorak with only latex gaskets at the wrist is a comfortable top, although it won't keep you dry in the event of a capsize.

Other Cold Weather Gear

There are few things as uncomfortable and annoying as cold feet, but luckily, there are many protection options to choose from. Neoprene booties with wool or neoprene socks provide the best defense against the cold.

You should also consider a warm hat, toque or skull-cap, and either pogies or neoprene mitts to keep your hands warm. Pogies attach to your paddle and allow you to slip your hands inside, which allows you to maintain direct contact with your paddle. Mitts are much warmer, but place a layer of neoprene between your hands and the paddle shaft,

The drysuit is the ultimate defense against the cold.

29

which some people have trouble getting used to.

The bottom line is that every day you'll need to assess the conditions and the likelihood of immersion, and then dress appropriately. If in doubt, wear an extra layer, as you're better off being too warm than too cold. Your kayak also has a ton of space for extra gear, so don't hesitate to bring extra clothing.

On a final note, remember that even on cold days, it's still important to protect yourself from the sun— so wear a hat, sunglasses, and use your sunscreen.

A wetsuit bootie will help keep your feet warm when wet.

SAFETY GEAR AND ACCESSORIES

Although kayaking is generally a very safe activity, there is always the potential for things to go wrong. If things do go awry, having the equipment on hand to quickly and efficiently deal with the situation can make a huge difference.

The following is a list of some standard safety equipment. Every situation is different and so before every trip you'll need to decide on what combination of safety gear makes the most sense. Because touring kayaks have so much cargo space there is no reason not to bring a full complement of safety gear. In particular, when you're paddling on the open ocean, there are a huge number of variables and there is less room for error than when paddling on lakes or rivers. If you're going to venture onto the ocean, it is highly recommended that you take a sea kayaking rescue course.

A first aid kit is important to bring on every sea kayak outing.

Water and Energy Bars

Since your body is the engine that drives your kayak forward, it's essential that it get enough fuel to do the job. A great strategy for staying energized and happy is to always bring along snacks like energy bars. I always have one or two in my PFD pocket. Arguably more important than food is water. Staying hydrated will keep you warm and feeling fit. The effects of dehydration are insidious and tend to sneak up on the unwary, but the good news is that dehydration is easy to avoid—you simply need to drink a lot of water, and to drink often. Hydration packs work incredibly well—when it's so easy to have a drink of water, there's no reason not to. Being fully hydrated may result in a few extra pit stops, but that's a very small price to pay for feeling good.

You wouldn't expect to drive anywhere on an empty tank, and for that same reason there's no reason to believe that you can paddle anywhere without fueling your body. Get into the habit of drinking and snacking often, especially while afloat. You'll feel stronger, happier, and maybe a little rounder too!

Spare Paddle

A spare paddle is always a good idea and simply a must if you are venturing onto the ocean, on multi-day trips, or when paddling in areas that don't leave you with any options but to paddle home. In a group setting, not every kayaker needs to have a spare paddle, although it's not a bad idea. As Murphy's Law states: if you don't bring it, you'll end up needing it.

Although your spare paddle doesn't have to be exactly the same as your main paddle, it should be good enough quality and have the same blade offset as your main paddle so that you'll be comfortable and confident when using it.

Your spare paddle must break down into two pieces, which can then be securely held under the deck rigging, with bungee cords over both the shaft and blades. Most paddlers prefer to store the paddle on the back deck—out of sight but within relatively easy reach from the cockpit.

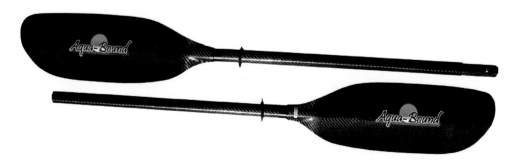

A spare paddle must break down into two-pieces so that it can be stored under the deck rigging.

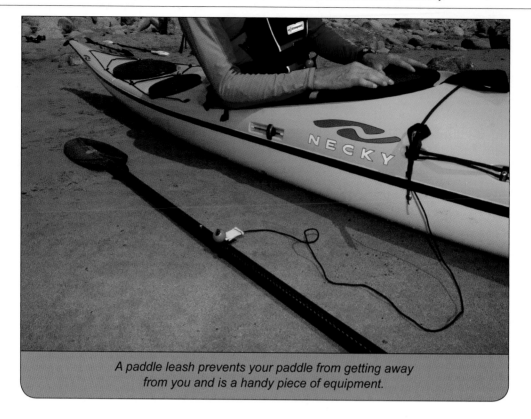

A paddle leash prevents your paddle from getting away from you and is a handy piece of equipment.

PADDLE LEASH

A paddle leash attaches your paddle to you or your boat, so that if you drop your paddle, you won't lose it. Leashes are great when taking photos, fishing, performing rescues, or in the event of a wet exit. Without a leash, even in broad daylight and calm conditions, it can be surprisingly difficult to spot and retrieve a paddle that has floated only a short distance away. In rougher or darker conditions, an errant paddle can disappear from sight in seconds and never be seen again.

There are two types of leashes: those that attach the paddle to the paddler, and the more popular system that connects the paddle to the boat. The best leashes are compact, simple designs that can be rolled up around the paddle shaft when not in use, or stored in a PFD pocket.

A couple of places to avoid the use of a paddle leash are in the surf zone or in strong current, where there is the potential danger of entanglement with the leash.

PUMP

Unless you paddle a sit-on-top kayak, you'll need a pump system to empty your boat of water should it become swamped. There are three types of pump systems: the hand pump, the deck-mounted pump, and the foot pump.

Hand pumps are the most popular because they're affordable and can be shared between paddlers. The downside of hand pumps is that it takes both hands to operate them, which can be tricky if you're alone or when you have wind or waves to contend with.

Deck-mounted and foot pumps both require serious modification to a kayak because the pump system is permanently bolted in place. A hose with a one-way valve allows you to pump water out of the boat, but doesn't let any in. The benefit of these systems is that you can use them with your skirt fully sealed, and they typically take only a single hand or foot to operate, which leaves you in a much better position to deal with prevailing conditions. The downside is that foot pumps (and some deck-mounted pumps) can't be shared with other kayakers, so on a group trip you may still need to bring a hand pump.

A hand pump is affordable and can be shared between paddlers.

EMERGENCY KIT

In many ways, day trips have the potential to be the most dangerous outings of all because paddlers generally won't be prepared for spending a night out. Of course, this can be a real problem if conditions conspire against you and force an impromptu night outside. The inability or unwillingness to spend a night out can then lead to very bad decision-making because 'heading home regardless of conditions' may seem like the only option.

A 20-liter dry bag makes a great emergency kit. Throw in a fleece jacket and pants, as well as a lightweight rain shell top and bottom, heavy wool socks, mittens and a hat, matches, fire starter, a headlamp, a bunch of energy bars, and even a compact tarp.

If you're paddling on a sheltered lake or on a river with plenty of access points, an emergency kit might not seem very important, but that's exactly why it's a good idea to bring one along! When paddling on the ocean, an emergency kit like the one described above should simply be considered an essential piece of gear.

FIRST AID KIT

Bringing a first aid kit on every trip is simple common sense, although it doesn't do much good if you don't know what's inside it or how to use the contents. This is especially important if you take part in multi-day trips, or find yourself acting as group leader. In these cases, it's a good idea to take a wilderness first aid course. You'll want to carry your first aid kit in a waterproof bag or container. Having the supplies in Zip-Lock bags inside a dry bag works well, as does using a Pelican case, or a Nalgene bottle with a wide mouth.

PADDLE FLOAT

A paddle float is a piece of rescue equipment designed to fit onto one blade of a paddle so that the blade will float and can then be used as an outrigger to stabilize the kayak. Paddle floats are helpful for a number of self-rescue techniques (all of which require training and practice to learn). If you haven't learned how to use a paddle float, it certainly doesn't mean that you can't paddle, but it does mean that it would be imprudent to paddle alone.

A paddle float attaches to your paddle blade so that you can lean on it against the water for support.

There are two basic types of paddle floats: inflatable and those made out of solid foam. Inflatable paddle floats have the advantage of being compact and providing a lot of buoyancy once full of air. The downside is that they are vulnerable to puncture and it takes time to inflate them before they can be used for rescue. This increases the amount of time that you spend in the water, which can be a real issue if the water is cold. Solid foam floats take up more room on the deck of your kayak and provide less buoyancy than inflatables, but they are far less prone to damage, and are quickly and easily deployed.

TOWLINE

A towline—as the name implies—is used by one paddler to help pull another paddler along. Towlines can be used to help a tired or seasick paddler make headway, and are extremely handy during some rescue situations.

Towlines are comprised of a belt that wraps around your waist or your PFD, a quick release buckle for breaking free, a leash that can either be short (5-10 feet), or long (30-45 feet), and a carabiner or hook on the end for clipping onto the boat that you're going to tow. Short towlines are sometimes called cow tails and are usually made of

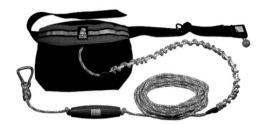

Towlines are an important piece of equipment that can be used to tow a tired or seasick paddler.

tubular webbing with an elastic shock cord inside to give both paddlers a smoother ride. Cow tails are quickly and easily deployed, but are only suitable for very short distance tows. Long towlines are generally made from floating line and are far better for towing over long distances. The long length provides much needed space between boats, so that the kayak under tow is unlikely to surf into the lead boat.

NAVIGATION TOOLS

Navigation tools are pieces of equipment that help you establish where you are on the water and how to get to where you want to go. Basic navigation is something that we all do instinctively (some better than others), and in many cases you won't need any real tools. For example, if you're on an isolated lake, you'll know that by following the shoreline one way or another, eventually you'll get back to where you started. Similarly, when paddling on a river, you'll know that if you paddled upstream to begin with, by heading downstream on that same side of the river you'll get back home. On the ocean, if you stick to one shoreline you can just turn around and head back home at any point. Although navigation tools aren't necessary in these cases, when you start dealing with more complicated marine geography they quickly become essential. In this book, only the very basics of navigation will be addressed. If you are interested in exploring the ocean, you'll want to take a navigation course and practice the skills that you learn. There's also an excellent book on the topic by Lee Moyer, called *Sea Kayaking Navigation Simplified*. Here is a quick overview of some of the more important navigation tools that you can learn to use.

Guidebooks

There are paddling-specific guidebooks available for many areas, and these are great resources. A good guidebook will include very valuable and detailed information on locations and points of interest. Some books even offer trip suggestions based on skill level and distance. If there's a guidebook available for the area that you're heading to, I would highly recommend picking it up.

Charts

Nautical charts are an amazing resource and your most important tool when it comes to navigation on the water. While *maps* are designed to supply information about

Nautical charts should be carried in waterproof chart cases.

what's on land, *charts* focus on the marine environment. When buying charts for an area, you'll have to consider what scale is most useful to you. The fine detail provided by large-scale charts affords better information for researching possible campsites and rest stops. Small-scale charts will give you a much better overview of your trip overall. You'll also need a waterproof chart case, which lets you store the chart under your fore deck rigging so that it is always in front of you.

Be aware that true marine charts are only available from licensed dealers. Any other guides or maps are not official charts, and will be labeled 'not for navigation'. Although many of these non-official charts are very useful to kayakers, none provide as much high-quality information as official charts.

Compass

The magnetic compass is another key navigation tool, but of course, they're only useful if you know how to use them. The best compasses for kayaking are dedicated marine compasses designed to mount on the fore deck of a boat.

Tide and Current Tables

Tides and currents can both have profound effects on sea conditions. Happily, both tides and tidal currents can be predicted with reasonable accuracy using tide and current tables, along with the appropriate marine charts.

GPS units

Handheld global positioning system (GPS) units are incredible pieces of technology that can tell you almost exactly where you are, using data from satellites. The only problem with them is that they rely entirely on batteries, and like any other piece of electronic equipment, are subject to failure in the field. For this reason, you don't want to be totally reliant on a GPS unit, to the exclusion of any other means of navigation (like the trusty old compass and chart).

GPS units require practice to use properly.

Watch

Believe it or not, the wristwatch is a useful piece of navigation equipment because relating distance to time is a key aspect of navigation. Simply put, you'll be able to know how far you've gone based on how fast and how long you've been paddling.

COMMUNICATION DEVICES

Communication Devices are tools that can help you stay in contact or help manage difficult situations, but it's important to note that they are not some sort of guarantee of safety, or a magical panacea that will automatically have the cavalry charging to your rescue. There are several communication devices available to the kayaker.

Cell Phones

Cell phones can really come in handy, but you can't rely on them fully because you never know when you'll be out of range or when your battery will run out of juice. Cell phones are also susceptible to failure from exposure to water.

Marine VHF

VHF radios provide one of the best means of signaling for help, because they can reach other boats in the area as well as the coast guard. You can also easily access marine weather forecasts and even make a phone call through a marine operator.

There is a strict operating protocol for these radios, designed to reduce channel

Marine VHF radios are among the best devices for emergency communication on the water.

overcrowding and to keep specific channels open to distress calls. Before you carry a VHF radio, make sure you learn about how to use it properly.

Satellite Phones

In truly remote areas, satellite phones will be your only option for communicating. While they are becoming more and more common, they are still very costly.

SIGNALING DEVICES

Signaling devices are used to get attention, and are usually reserved for emergencies.

Whistles

A whistle is one of the best ways to get someone's attention. Use three short and powerful blasts to signal an emergency, and a single blast to simply draw attention.

Mirrors

Mirrors are used to signal others by reflecting the light of the sun at the target. Many signaling mirrors are little more than a polished metal surface, which makes them virtually unbreakable. Some have a hole so that you can look through the mirror and more accurately aim its reflective surface.

Flares

Flares are like small fireworks or rockets that are launched into the sky. Flares are most visible on overcast days and especially at night. The best flares for kayakers are called pen flares, which are small enough that they can easily be stored in a PFD pocket. Flares expire over time, and have an expiration date stamped on them. Each paddler should carry a minimum of three flares to maximize chances of being seen by rescuers.

Smoke

Smoke canisters provide another means of signaling. Although smoke can be very effective in daylight, at night it is useless. Smoke also doesn't work well in windy conditions.

Strobes

A strobe is a very bright flashing light. Strobes can be attached to the shoulder of your PFD to attract attention at night or in low light, but they should only ever be activated in an emergency, because on the water a strobe represents a mayday signal.

CHAPTER TWO

BEFORE HITTING THE WATER

**CARING FOR YOUR KAYAK • TRANSPORTING YOUR KAYAK
GETTING IN & OUT • SITTING IN A KAYAK
PUTTING ON THE SPRAY SKIRT • USING YOUR PADDLE**

CARING FOR YOUR KAYAK

Kayaks really are pretty simple vehicles and don't require a whole lot of maintenance, but there are a few things you can do to prolong your boat's life. One of the simpler ways to keep your boat looking good and working smoothly is to rinse it with fresh water after it's been in salt water, paying special attention to any moving parts like the rudder or skeg, cables, and pedals. For composite boats, applying a good marine wax will also help protect your boat from salt and from the sun's damaging UV radiation.

One of the most important things you can do for your boat is to store it properly. Ideally, it should be stored on its side, supported at the bulkheads. If you're storing it outside, keep it out of direct sunlight and make sure that it's turned over so that no water can get in and fill the boat over time. Water weighs a lot, and if left in a boat for extended periods, it can do real damage. It's also a good idea to leave the hatches off to let air circulate in the boat, allow the hatches to dry out, and keep hatch seals as new and tight as possible.

Something else to keep in mind is that it's actually quite normal for the hull of plastic boats to deform a bit over time. If your boat gets some serious warping or dents, heat will often be enough to return the kayak to its original shape. On a hot day, the sun alone can do the trick, but if that doesn't work, you can dump some hot water into the kayak and encourage some of the dents out.

TRANSPORTING YOUR KAYAK

For very short distances you'll be able to carry your kayak by hand, although you may need the help of a friend. If the distance is too far to comfortably carry your kayak, but short enough for an enjoyable walk, a kayak cart works very well. A kayak cart supports one end of your kayak and has a couple of wheels so that you can easily pull it behind you. For longer distances, a vehicle is your only option.

CARRYING YOUR KAYAK

The unfortunate truth is that sea kayaks are cumbersome on land and a pain to carry. Even composite kayaks—which are quite a bit lighter than plastic ones—are tricky to carry simply because kayaks are so long.

Unless there's no choice, you'll want to carry your boat instead of dragging it. For many, this means that moving a boat around is a two-person job. For stronger individuals, a kayak can be carried on the shoulder. The challenge is usually in getting it there. To get a kayak onto your shoulder, make sure you bend your legs and keep your back as straight as possible. Start by lifting the boat onto your thighs with the cockpit out, and then roll it up onto your shoulder.

When a kayak is loaded, a solo carry is not an option. If you're in a group, get everyone to pitch in to help, with the strongest at the ends and the others gripping the cockpit coaming to help carry the load.

Whether you're doing a solo or tandem carry, you'll be walking around with 16 to 20 feet of kayak. Take corners wide and make sure that other people know you're coming through.

LOADING & UNLOADING YOUR KAYAK

It doesn't take a rocket scientist to figure out that strapping an 18-foot kayak to the roof of your vehicle can be a real recipe for disaster.

When it comes to car-topping, you really need to have a good, solid set of roof racks, and unfortunately, most factory installed racks on vehicles aren't up to the task. Yakima and Thule are both leaders in the field of vehicle rack systems and they have a number of great designs that make loading and unloading kayaks surprisingly easy.

Loading a boat is much easier with two people—one at each end. If you've got a high roof, you might consider

First lift the boat onto your thighs.

Roll the boat onto your shoulder.

Rest the cockpit coaming on your shoulder and grab the thigh hook for more support.

Specialized rollers and cradles are the ultimate roof top rack systems.

getting racks with rollers that let you slide the kayak on. There are also boat cradles available, which attach to the rack and provide the cushiest ride for your kayak. Otherwise, use foam to pad out the racks where they will contact your boat(s). If you are carrying more than one kayak, be sure to keep them from rubbing against each other by spacing them out, or by placing a piece of foam between them.

TYING YOUR KAYAK DOWN

To tie a boat down to your roof racks, ropes work fine, but straps are best. They're quicker, easier, and you won't find yourself dealing with anyone's 'death knot'. As long as you don't strap it down at its widest point, your kayak will probably not fly off your roof, even if it's tied on a little loosely, so don't feel that you need to crank the boat down with all your might. Straps need to be snug, but you don't want to crush the boat. At the same time, you can expect that your tying job will loosen after driving for a while, so be sure to check the straps or ropes every so often.

It's also a good idea to tie a bowline or stern line to your kayak for extra security. If you do this, make sure you don't tie them too tightly, which will flex the ends of your kayak downwards and put unnecessary strain on its structure. Always make sure that there are no loose ends that could be caught in the car's wheels.

Generally, it is the responsibility of the driver to ensure that all kayaks are effectively secured to the roof of the vehicle. If you're the driver, make sure that after boats are tied down, you double and triple check everything. Don't pull away until you're completely satisfied that the load is safely secured. Losing a kayak off the roof of a vehicle is a very scary thing, and a serious hazard to everyone on the road.

Bow and stern lines provide added security but they should not be over-tightened.

GETTING IN AND OUT

There are lots of different ways to get into a kayak. The only real rule is to 'get your butt into the boat quickly'. It's that awkward transition between standing and sitting where 99% of the carnage occurs.

FROM A DOCK

Getting into a kayak from a dock can be tricky, especially from higher docks. You're best off getting the help of one of your friends to hold the boat while you get in. If you're the last person getting on the water, one of your friends can pull up alongside your kayak and help stabilize it from there. Either way, start by floating your kayak in close, alongside the dock, and then sit on the dock and place your feet in the cockpit. Keep your weight on the dock and make sure that your feet are close to the centerline of the hull. Rotating towards the bow of your boat, get a good grip on the dock with both hands, and then lower yourself into the seat while sliding your legs into the boat. Get

Keep a good grip on the dock when getting in.

Ideally, you'll get in so that it only takes a couple of little pushes on the sand to take off.

into the habit of placing your paddle within easy reach, so you'll be able to grab it once you're in your boat.

Getting out involves the same steps, but in reverse. Once again, it will be very helpful to have one of your paddling friends stabilize your kayak either from the dock or from their kayak.

ON A BEACH

If you're getting into your kayak on a beach, you can do so with your boat resting on the sand. You can then push yourself out in the water or have a friend give you a push. Of course, it makes sense to do this as close to the water as possible. Ideally, you'll be able to get into your kayak in an inch or two of water so that it only takes a couple of little pushes to take off.

Getting into and out of your kayak on a beach that has surf is a bit trickier and is something that we'll look at in the 'Paddling in Surf' section of this book.

ON ROCKY SHORE

On rocky launch sites, where sliding in from shore could damage your kayak, the best way to get into your kayak involves floating your kayak in the water and then using your paddle as an outrigger for stability. This is done by placing your paddle at ninety degrees to the kayak with one blade on shore and with the shaft resting on the boat behind the cockpit. While putting your weight onto the outrigger for support, grasp the paddle behind your

Rest your paddle behind the cockpit
and use it as an outrigger for support.

Stay low and grip your paddle
firmly as you step into your kayak.

Keep your weight on the outrigger side
of the kayak as you slide your legs in.

You can get out using this
same technique.

back, squat down beside the kayak, and then slip your legs into the boat. Throughout the maneuver, be sure to maintain a slight lean onto the outrigger side of the kayak to avoid flipping in the opposite direction.

You can get out of your kayak on uneven or rocky shorelines using this same technique in reverse, although it will be difficult if you have any surf to contend with.

Sit upright in the kayak, with your knees flexed comfortably and splayed out under the thigh hooks.

SITTING IN A KAYAK

As a general rule, your boat should fit like a good pair of shoes: snug yet comfortable.

When sitting in your kayak, your legs should be in front of you with your knees flexed and legs splayed out and under the thigh hooks. Your feet should be resting comfortably and securely against the foot pedals, and the back band should be supporting your lower back, encouraging an upright sitting position, but not preventing you from leaning back.

Your kayak will probably not provide the greatest fit straight 'off the rack' and will likely require a little custom tailoring to yield the best fit possible.

CUSTOMIZING YOUR KAYAK

The seating position in a kayak provides five important points of contact with the boat: feet, legs, butt, hips, and lower back. By maximizing your fit and comfort at all these key points, you will greatly increase your control over your kayak.

Foot Support: Pedal systems in kayaks are designed for easy customization and slide on a track to accommodate paddlers of different leg lengths. Adjust your foot pedals so that when you're seated in your kayak, the balls of your feet are firmly planted on the pedals, with your legs comfortably bent and your knees tucked under the deck.

Leg Support: If we look at boat control, thigh hooks are the single most important piece of outfitting. Thigh hooks are designed to wrap over your upper leg, providing a surface to squeeze against for support and to pull up against for edging. Your legs should fit comfortably under the thigh hooks with even pressure across your thigh. Some paddlers will also glue foam to the inside of the kayak to provide support under and beside the legs. This can provide additional control and help reduce hip discomfort.

Butt Support: Although your butt is one of the most padded parts of your body, it will still appreciate a little tender loving care. Many seats now come padded in some way, but if yours isn't padded, you can easily glue a thin sheet of foam down. Most seats also come contoured. This helps to spread your weight over the widest area and also prevents your butt from sliding around in the boat. Unfortunately, butts come in all shapes and sizes, so you may still need to glue some foam to the seat and then shape it. Don't get too carried away building up your seat though, because the higher you sit in the boat, the less stable you'll feel.

Hip Support: The seat should also provide contact with your hips, and foam hip pads are the most comfortable solution. Hip pads will prevent sliding side-to-side and give you the most control over the edging of your kayak. Different boats provide different solutions for hip pads, although you may need to simply glue foam in and shape it around your hips.

Lower Back Support: Having some form of back support will keep your butt from sliding around, promote good posture and paddling technique, and will help make your time on the water far more comfortable. Back bands are by and large the most functional and effective systems, although some kayak seats have a rigid seatback instead. Back support should be snug against the lower back, encouraging an erect sitting position, and an active posture, but not impede your ability to lean right back.

OUTFITTING TIP

For padding, closed-cell foam (also referred to as mini-cell foam) is a wonderful material that absorbs no water, is easily shaped, and provides a firm yet pliant surface to press against. To attach foam in place, prepare the surfaces of both the boat and the foam by roughening them with coarse sandpaper, and then use contact cement to glue the pads in. You can then shape the foam to a custom fit with a serrated knife, sandpaper or with a Sureform. Make sure that all your outfitting is secure in the kayak, so that if you capsize it won't be washed away.

Having emphasized the need for a good, snug, comfortable fit, it's equally important to note that you should never, under any circumstances, do anything that will impede your ability to wet-exit a kayak or easily re-enter it from the water.

PUTTING ON THE SPRAY SKIRT

Putting on the skirt can be extremely frustrating in the beginning, especially if you're using a neoprene skirt that makes a tight seal. The best way to get your skirt on is to sit upright, and start from the back. You'll then work the skirt onto the coaming around to your hips, where you can often pin it down with your forearms as you grab the front of the skirt and stretch it over the front of the coaming. The sides of the skirt will then pop on very easily. Make sure that when you pull the front of the skirt on that you leave the pull-tab out, because you'll need it to get the skirt off when the time comes to exit the boat.

If you're having trouble getting a neoprene skirt snapped on your boat try wetting it first. Neoprene becomes more flexible and pliable when it's wet. If you still can't get the skirt on, or can't reliably pop it off by yanking on the pull-tab, then get a different skirt.

USING YOUR PADDLE

As you spend more time in a kayak, and your skills improve, your paddle will evolve into a natural extension of your arms. We've already discussed how to choose a paddle, so now let's look at how to use it.

For kayakers who favor an unfeathered paddle (blades not offset), once the grip on the shaft is established for both hands, it shouldn't change dramatically regardless of the stroke. To establish your grip, align your knuckles with the plane of the blade. Your hands should be a little more than shoulder width apart. You can check your grip both by looking out at your hands and by lifting your paddle up onto your head. With the shaft across your noggin, the angle that your arms are bent at should be about 90 degrees. This hand placement gives you the best combination of control and power.

For kayakers who prefer a feathered paddle, the grip is a little more complicated. Being left or right-handed has an important impact on your paddling, as it dictates which is your control hand. Quite simply, for a right-handed paddler, the control hand is the right; for a left-handed paddler, the control hand is the left. Your 'control' hand is the hand that grips the shaft securely at all times, which is why it's also called the 'glue' hand. The control hand's grip should never change, whether you're forward paddling, back paddling, bracing, rolling, or doing anything else. The other hand is

When using a feathered paddle, your 'control' hand keeps a firm grip while the 'grease' hand is loose enough to allow the shaft to rotate within it.

As the 'control' hand lifts, the 'grease' hand allows the shaft to rotate.

often referred to as the 'grease' hand and has a looser grip to allow the shaft to rotate within it. After taking a stroke with the blade on the side of your control hand, loosen your grip with the other hand and let the shaft rotate. This rotation is necessary to accommodate the 'feather', or 'twist' of your paddle, and lets you place the next blade in the water squarely. Of course, the less feather that your paddle has, the less you'll be rotating the shaft in your grease hand.

Whatever your paddle's feather angle, your grip on the paddle should be secure but light. An overly tight grip will only lead to sore forearms and potential tendonitis.

CHAPTER THREE

THE ESSENTIALS

WET EXIT • THREE GOLDEN RULES• PADDLING POSTURE
EDGING A KAYAK • BRACES • USING A RUDDER OR SKEG

WET EXIT

A wet exit refers to the act of getting out of your kayak when it's upside down, and it's one of the first skills that any paddler should learn.

To smoothly exit an overturned kayak, the first thing you'll do is lean forward and find your skirt's rip cord with one hand, while the other hand firmly hangs on to your paddle. Now yank the ripcord forward and up to pop your skirt. Next, slide your hands back to your hips (still holding the paddle), and while staying leaning forward, push yourself out. You'll end up doing a bit of a forward somersault out of the boat.

The trickiest part of this maneuver is fighting the instinct to lean back as you slide out of your kayak. The problem with leaning back is that it raises your butt off the seat and presses your thighs against the thigh hooks, which will actually make it harder to

Keep hold of your paddle as you pull the ripcord to pop your skirt.

Stay leaning forward as you push yourself out of the kayak.

You'll end up doing a somersault out of the boat.

Grab hold of your kayak as soon as you're out.

slide out, and slow down your wet exit.

The entire process of wet exiting will only take a few seconds, and the more relaxed you are, the more smoothly it'll all go. The first few times it may feel as if you'll soon be short of air, but in reality you have lots of time, so relax and practice sitting there for a few moments before popping out of the boat. Once you're out, immediately grab your boat and make sure you still have your paddle. Keeping gear together will greatly speed up any rescue process.

THREE GOLDEN RULES

The 'Three Golden Rules' distill three absolutely key concepts of paddling mechanics that every kayaker should use, regardless of the type of paddling that they do. You must have a co-operative division of your body, you must maintain a power position with your arms, and you must harness the power of torso rotation.

#1 CO-OPERATIVE DIVISION OF THE BODY

The co-operative division of the body is just a fancy way of saying that while your upper body performs one task, your lower body can perform a totally separate one. For example, your upper body may be actively driving your kayak forward while your lower body is holding your boat on edge. Your lower and upper bodies can be doing two totally separate things, but still be working together in concert. It's like playing the drums: your hands do one thing while your feet do another.

Your lower and upper body should work independently yet co-operatively with each other.

#2 MAINTAIN THE POWER POSITION

Sea kayaking is generally a very safe sport, but unfortunately injuries do still occur. The most common injuries are minor ones that stem from overuse, like blisters or tendonitis. Unfortunately, shoulder dislocation is not very unusual either, and is a far more serious injury that you need to be wary of—especially if you're paddling in more challenging conditions. One of the best ways to prevent injuries is by maintaining a "power position" with your arms.

The power position simply involves keeping your hands in front of your body. This is important because if one of your hands gets behind you, then your arm is in a very vulnerable position.

Another way to think of the power position is to picture your arms, chest and paddle forming a box when your paddle is held out in front of you. This box is the cornerstone of the power position, and should be maintained throughout all maneuvers.

So does this mean that you can't reach to the back of your boat to take a stroke? No. What it means is that in order to reach to the back of your boat you'll need to rotate your whole upper body so that your hands stay in front of you. This act of rotating the upper body is fittingly called torso rotation. It not only keeps your shoulders safe, but also lets you harness the most power for all your strokes, which is why it's our Third Golden Rule!

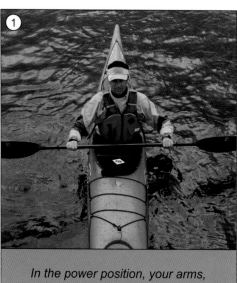

In the power position, your arms, chest and paddle form a box.

By rotating your whole upper body, you can maintain your power position when reaching for a stroke at the stern.

#3 TORSO ROTATION

Your paddle strokes need to use much more than just your arm and shoulder muscles. To harness the potential of your whole body, you'll need the power of torso rotation. Torso rotation is the way you get your front and side stomach muscles involved with your strokes. Using these larger muscles will let you paddle harder, for longer, because your efforts will be spread over more and larger muscles.

There are three components to torso rotation: the winding up of the body, the planting of the paddle blade, and the unwinding of the body.

Winding up the body means turning your upper body at the waist so your chest no longer faces the direction that your kayak does. Once your body is wound up, plant your paddle in the water as a pivot. As you push or pull on the pivot blade, your stomach muscles can pull your body back to its position of rest. The act of using your stomach muscles to return your body to its position of rest is referred to as unwinding the body. Think of your body as an elastic band. The more you wind it up, the more power you'll have available to you as it unwinds.

PADDLING POSTURE

Paddling posture refers to the different ways your body positioning can help with the control and balance of your kayak. As with any sport, posture plays an important role in paddling performance.

The ideal sitting position in a kayak is upright; the same way that Mom always told you to sit at the dinner table! This doesn't mean that you can't lean backwards or forwards when the situation calls for it, but sitting upright should be your default body position. An upright posture will give you the most control over your boat's edging, let you rotate your upper body the most effectively, and give your strokes the most power.

Good posture when paddling means sitting up straight.

It's also very important that you keep your upper body balanced over the kayak. In flatwater this isn't so hard, but when you start dealing with waves, or current, you need to let your boat tilt without your upper body doing the same. The key is to follow the first Golden Rule by staying loose in the hips and letting your boat rock from edge to edge while your upper body stays upright.

A good way to get used to keeping your hips loose is to rock your boat from edge to edge, while keeping your upper body as quiet as possible. Pretend that you're holding a tray with your favorite drink on it, and that you don't want to spill a drop.

EDGING A KAYAK

No matter what type of paddling you'll be doing, the way to take your skills to the next level is to become proficient and comfortable with balancing your kayak on edge. Most notably, you can edge your kayak to make quick turns, or to keep your kayak on course, even when confronted with wind, waves, currents, or all three at once. Furthermore, the concept behind edging your kayak is the same concept that allows you to stay upright when conditions get rough.

When tilting your boat on edge, remember to keep your hips loose and your weight balanced over your kayak. Now shift your weight slightly over to one butt cheek and lift the opposite knee. You should feel your whole rib cage shifting over to the side

To edge your kayak, keep your upper body upright as you shift your weight over to one butt cheek and lift your opposite knee. Your head needs to stay over your kayak.

of your kayak. Your stomach and side muscles will be working to keep your body upright, while your legs hold a steady tilt on your boat.

As you progress, it's important that you develop the ability to transfer from edge to edge comfortably and quickly. This is a great skill to practice on flatwater, or even while forward paddling, which we'll be looking at later.

BRACES

No matter how good your balance is, sometimes you will lose it. A brace is a stroke used to recover when you've been thrown off balance. There are two basic forms of braces: the 'high' and 'low' brace. Both involve reaching out to the side of your kayak with your paddle and slapping the water with one blade, which provides the support needed for your body to right the boat. The only real difference between the two is the position of your paddle. It's critical to understand that the slap of the paddle just provides momentary support. It's your body that's responsible for the rest. Let's take a quick look at how it does this.

As you flip, the only way to right the kayak is by pulling up with the knee that is going underwater. The only way to pull up with this bottom knee is to drop your head towards the water in the direction that you're flipping. Doing this is extremely counter-intuitive, but it's absolutely essential. Your head should be the last thing to come back up on a well-executed brace. If, instead, you lift your head up, you'll inadvertently pull on your top knee, which simply flips you even more quickly. To make sure that your head drops towards the water, try watching your slapping blade as you brace. It's hard to lift your head if you're looking down.

LOW BRACE

The low brace is so named because the paddle is kept very low. To set your paddle up for a low brace, sit upright and roll the paddle under your elbows so that your forearms are virtually vertical. Think of a pushup position. From here, you'll reach out to 90 degrees so that one hand is at your belly button and the other is out over the water. You'll then smack the water with the non power-face or backside of your paddle blade. Practice slapping the water on alternating sides, making sure that your paddle hits the water flat. If your paddle has any type of feather, you'll need to rotate your the paddle in your grease hand in order to slap the water with a flat backside of your blade. After slapping the water, slide your paddle forward and inward, and roll your knuckles upward to clear the blade from the water.

When you get comfortable with these moves with your boat sitting flat on the water, start edging the boat slightly in the direction that you brace. As you slap the water,

1

The low brace uses the backside of your paddle in a pushup position.

2

Slapping the water with a flat blade provides momentary support.

3

Drop your head and level off the kayak by pulling up with your lower knee.

4

Slide the paddle forward and roll your knuckles upward to clear the blade from the water.

drop your head in that direction and pull up with your lower knee to level off the kayak. Keep practicing these motions until they feel natural, and then start pushing your boat tilts further and further.

The low brace is a great reactionary brace that can be thrown in at less than a second's notice. Once you're comfortable with it, the low brace will become your best recovery technique, and it also keeps your shoulders well-protected from injury.

HIGH BRACE

The high brace is definitely the most powerful of the recovery techniques. A good paddler can even use the high brace to recover when their boat is almost completely upside down! The problem with the high brace is that it's easy to rely on it too much, which can put your shoulders at risk. So the first thing to keep in mind is that despite its name, you need to keep your paddle and your hands low and in front of your body.

Otherwise, the high brace follows the same rules as the low brace; only for the high brace you'll use your paddle in a 'chin-up' position, instead of the 'push-up' position. This means you'll be using the power-face instead of the backside of your blades to contact the water.

Starting with a flat boat, keep your elbows low and roll your paddle up until your forearms are almost vertical. You'll now reach out over the water at 90 degrees, with your inside arm low, in what is sometimes called the 'nose pick' position. It's important that this hand stay low so that your paddle blade is as flat to the water surface as possible when it makes contact, offering you the most support. After slapping the water, slide your paddle inward, roll your knuckles forward and slice the blade out of the water.

Once you're comfortable high bracing on both sides, start tilting your boat slightly, and combine the head drop and knee pull-up with your motions. This means that as you slap the water, you'll drop your head towards the water and pull up with your

The high brace uses the power face of your paddle in a low, chin-up position.

Slap the water with a flat blade to get momentary support.

Drop your head and level off the kayak by pulling up with your lower knee.

Keep your hands low throughout the high brace to keep your shoulders safe.

lower knee to right the kayak. Remember that looking at your active blade is a good habit to get into as it helps keep your head down.

As you perfect the high brace, you'll be amazed at powerful it can be. Just remember that for even the biggest high braces, you've got to keep your hands low to keep your shoulders safe from injury.

USING A RUDDER OR SKEG

Although it may initially seem confusing, rudders and skegs aren't actually used to make a kayak turn—they're there to help the boat go straight. In high winds, strong currents or any other challenging conditions, it can be very difficult to keep a kayak running straight, as the boat will constantly be deflected and knocked off course. Skegs and rudders both help a kayak stay on course, but each system works differently.

Rudders flip down from their stored position on deck, by means of haul lines found

The effects of deploying a skeg at varying depths.

alongside, or just aft, of the cockpit. Because rudders swivel side to side, they are incredibly powerful when it comes to keeping a kayak on course. But bear in mind that for a rudder to exert any effect, the boat must be moving. Because sliding pedals inside the cockpit control the rudder, a paddler can easily make course corrections by trimming the rudder angle with their feet. They can do so while continuing to paddle forward with no disruption to paddling power or rhythm (another great example of the co-operative division of upper and lower body). To turn to the right, the right foot is extended. To turn to the left, the left foot is extended. Rudders are unbeatable in following seas, helping to control surfs, and often preventing the deflection of the bow.

Skegs are typically deployed using a slider mechanism located on deck by the paddler's knee. The depth of the skeg is set by fine adjustments to the position of the slider. A good sea kayak is designed to weathercock, or turn bow into the wind. By deploying the skeg, the balance of a boat can be changed. The depth of the skeg determines how much surface area is introduced into the water at the stern of the kayak, and dictates how much effect the skeg will have. A fully retracted skeg should allow a kayak to turn into the wind. A fully deployed skeg should cause the kayak to rotate down wind, pivoting at the skeg blade. A carefully deployed skeg will achieve the perfect balance for the conditions and allow the boat to hold a straight course far more easily.

CHAPTER FOUR

THE ESSENTIAL STROKES

FORWARD STROKE • FORWARD PADDLING ON EDGE • BACK STROKE
SWEEP STROKES • STOPPING • DRAW STROKE • STERN RUDDER
BOW DRAW • LOW BRACE LEAN TURN • HIGH BRACE LEAN TURN

FORWARD STROKE

The forward stroke is the single most important stroke, and often the least understood. Since 99% of touring consists of paddling forward, we're going to spend some time looking at the mechanics of this essential stroke, and pinpoint ways to make it more efficient. The bottom line is that unless you're racing, any stroke that gets your kayak moving is fine, but by improving your forward stroke you'll be able to paddle faster, longer, and in greater comfort.

The forward stroke can be broken down into three parts: catch, rotation, and recovery.

THE CATCH

The catch is the all-important start to the stroke, where you place your paddle blade in the water. Sitting up straight, with a relaxed grip on your paddle, reach to your toes and plant your blade fully in the water. This reaching action involves both your arms and your shoulders. Do not lean forward at the waist to reach to your toes, but rather twist from the waist. If you're reaching for a stroke with your right blade, you'll push your right shoulder forward while reaching with your right arm. This shoulder-reach causes you to rotate your upper torso or 'wind-up' your body. As we already know, this torso rotation lets you harness the power of your front and side stomach muscles for strokes, rather than just using your arms. With your body wound up, spear your blade into the water so that the whole blade is submerged. Once that blade is completely in the water, pull on your paddle and unwind your upper body to drive your boat forward.

One of the most common mistakes is pulling on the forward stroke before the blade is fully planted in the water. If you're doing this, you'll notice your strokes creating a lot of splash, which means that you're actually wasting energy pulling water past your kayak, rather than pulling your kayak forward through the water. To understand this better, imagine that you're planting your paddle in cement when you take a stroke. The paddle shouldn't really move anywhere once it's planted. Instead, you're pulling yourself past that paddle. The only way this will work is if you have fully and securely planted your whole blade in the water.

ROTATION

Your body is like a powerful spring once it's wound up, and you'll have a lot of potential energy at your command. Rotation refers to the way you'll use this energy to power your forward stroke.

As described above, after the catch, your body should be wound up and your paddle firmly planted at your toes. You'll now pull on your paddle and drive your kayak forward using as much of your large torso muscles as possible, rather than relying on your comparatively weak arms to do the work. In fact, a good way to think about this is that your arms are just a supplement to the power of your torso. True power comes from your stomach, side, and back muscles. To get a feel for this, try a few strokes paddling forward with your arms locked straight at the elbows. It may not be comfortable to paddle like this, but you can really get your boat moving—and the only way to do it is with pronounced torso rotation.

Now that you're engaging the most powerful muscles, let's take a quick look at what the rest of your body will be doing. With elbows bent and staying low, pull on the paddle with your arms as you take each stroke. The range of motion for your arms will be quite small since your torso will be doing the bulk of the work. As a general rule, the more vertical the paddle shaft is while taking a forward stroke, the more power you're getting from it. To get the paddle more vertical, bring your top hand higher and further across your boat. These high top-hand strokes are great when you're in a hurry, but they're also very tiring. For a long day of paddling, where endurance is more important, keep your top hand about shoulder or chest level.

For maximum drive, your legs can

Plant your paddle blade firmly in the water at your toes before pulling.

Notice the arms move very little as the stroke is pulled through. The power comes from torso rotation.

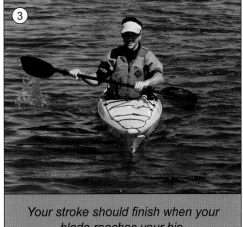

Your stroke should finish when your blade reaches your hip.

also be involved with your forward stroke. By pushing off the foot peg on the same side that you're taking a stroke on, you will transfer as much rotational power as possible to driving the kayak forward.

RECOVERY

The recovery is the point at which your forward stroke ends and the blade is removed from the water. This happens at your hip, which is earlier than most paddlers think. When your stroke reaches your hip, slice your paddle out of the water sideways and get ready for the next stroke. At this point, your body should have unwound past its position of rest, and be wound up, ready to catch your other blade on the opposite side. So spear your blade deeply into the water, and then pull the next stroke through.

Now that you have all the pieces for an efficient and powerful forward stroke, try to put them all together as smoothly as possible while keeping your boat as quiet as you can. A 'quiet' boat has minimal bob from side to side or up and down, and will let your kayak glide through the water the most efficiently.

FORWARD PADDLING ON EDGE

Once you have a confident and efficient forward stroke, a great thing to practice is paddling forward with your boat held on edge. A great drill for improving this skill is to paddle in a straight line, switching from one edge to the other after about 10 strokes on each side. With practice, you should be able to paddle forward while holding your kayak on a steady edge without any wobbles or bracing.

What you'll immediately discover when doing this is that your kayak has a tendency to turn away from

Paddling with your boat on edge is a great skill to practice.

the direction that you're tilting your boat. The more you tilt your kayak, the more aggressively your kayak will turn. This handling characteristic will be useful when making small adjustments, or when you have wind or currents trying to sweep you off course.

BACK STROKE

Although you won't use the back stroke all that often, it will become more important as you improve and begin to paddle in rougher conditions. In many ways, the back stroke is fairly intuitive, but steering while going backwards is definitely not. The only way to get comfortable paddling backwards is by practicing, and you're best off doing so in a controlled environment.

The back stroke really is the forward stroke in reverse. First off, you'll use the back face of your paddle, so fight the urge to change your grip on your paddle or rotate your paddle in your hands. Like the forward stroke, your torso rotation provides the real power for the back stroke and your arms are just a power supplement. The stroke enters the water just behind your hip and ends at your toes, while your top hand is held in front of your body between chest and chin height. As you plant your blade deeply in the water behind your hip, turn your chest aggressively in that same direction. This effectively winds up your body. Now, as you push on your blade, unwind your body and drive your back shoulder forward until your paddle reaches your toes. At this point, your body should be wound up in the other direction. Slice that blade out of the water and drop the other blade into the water just behind your other hip.

1

The back stroke is planted firmly in the water, just behind your hip.

2

Torso rotation provides much of the power for the stroke.

3

Finish the back stroke at your toes, without over extending your arms.

SWEEP STROKES

Most sea kayaks are designed to travel forward efficiently in a straight line, so you can't expect them to turn on a dime. But there are times when you will need to make a quick turn, and the sweep stroke will help you do just that.

FORWARD SWEEP

The forward sweep stroke can be used while stationary, or while moving. The nice thing about using it while moving is that it lets you turn your boat effectively while keeping your forward speed going.

Like the forward stroke, the forward sweep stroke starts with your body wound up and your blade completely in the water at your toes. It also harnesses the power of

The forward sweep starts with your body wound up and your paddle planted deeply at your toes with the shaft held low.

Keeping your hands low, sweep an arcing path far out to the side of the kayak.

Following your active blade with your eyes helps incorporate torso rotation into the stroke.

Finish your sweep before your paddle hits your kayak and return to your starting position with your paddle ready in a low brace.

your torso rotation. Unlike the forward stroke, your hands will stay low and your blade will follow an arcing path as far out to the side of your kayak as possible. It will continue on this path until it's about six inches from the stern of your kayak. Make sure to slice your blade out before your stroke touches the stern or your paddle will get pinned against the kayak, making you very unstable and potentially capsizing the boat.

As you perform this stroke, watch your blade and rotate your upper body through the stroke. Be sure to 'finish the stroke'—complete the sweeping arc of your paddle—because this last third of the stroke is the most important part for turning the boat.

The recovery for this stroke is done in a low brace position. As you rewind your torso to repeat the stroke, or to return to a neutral position, the back of the paddle blade sweeps across the water as a low brace, ready to be deployed should you lose your balance and need a little extra support. When skimming your blade across the water during the recovery phase, keep the leading edge of your blade angled upward to create lift, and to prevent the paddle from diving.

REVERSE SWEEP

The reverse sweep is exactly what it sounds like—a forward sweep stroke done in reverse, and like the back stroke, you'll use the back face of your paddle. The reverse sweep can be used while stationary, or when traveling forward, although it's important to note that it will kill almost all of your speed. For this reason it can be helpful when you need to put on the brakes and make a major course correction.

With your hands low and in the power position in front of your body, wind your body up by turning aggressively and watching your paddle enter the water at the stern of your kayak. With your blade planted deeply in the water, sweep a full, wide arc all the way to your toes, with your head following the blades progression, and your body unwinding aggressively.

Once you've finished the stroke, you'll want to return to a neutral position, or if performing another reverse sweep on the same side, you'll need to rewind your torso for the next stroke. The recovery for the reverse sweep stroke is done in a high brace position. As you rotate back to your starting position, the power face of your paddle blade will sweep over the surface of the water, ready as a brace if needed. When skimming your blade across the water during the recovery phase, keep the leading edge of your blade angled upward to create lift, and to prevent the paddle from diving.

The reverse sweep starts at the stern of your kayak with your head and body aggressively rotated towards it.

Sweep a wide arc with your paddle with your hands kept low.

Notice the arms have stayed in a relatively fixed position throughout the stroke, which means torso rotation was providing much of the power.

The stroke ends after having swept a full, wide arc.

SWEEPING ON EDGE

As described in the section on 'Edging a Kayak', putting your kayak on edge lets it turn more easily. So, once you're comfortable sweeping with your boat kept flat, it's time to add some boat tilt to the equation to make your sweep stroke its most effective.

Whether you're using a forward or reverse sweep stroke, the further you tilt your kayak, the more effectively you'll turn. Of course, holding your boat on edge is a balancing act and so what you can do to stay upright is change the angle that your blade sweeps through the water, so that it provides bracing support as you unwind your body. Think of your sweep as a modified brace. If your blade is angled at about 45 degrees, it will provide a good mix of support and turning power.

Putting this into context, let's assume that you want to turn your kayak to the right, which means that you'll either be using a forward sweep on the left, or a reverse sweep on the right. If you're using a forward sweep on the left, you'll tilt your boat to the left, towards the stroke. In this case, you'll cock your wrists back slightly so that your blade is angled at 45 degrees through the sweep. If you're using a reverse sweep on the right, you'll tilt your boat to the right, into your stroke, and you'll cock your wrists back slightly to establish a 45 degree angle on the blade sweeping forward.

The recovery phase for edged sweeps doesn't change at all, although it does become more important that you are ready to brace if required.

Once you're comfortably doing forward and reverse sweeps with your boat on edge, try combining the two (forward sweep on one side and reverse sweep on the other). As a combination, this is the quickest way to turn your kayak, and will allow you to virtually spin a boat in place.

Your kayak will turn more quickly when tilted into your sweep.

A low brace recovery is used after the forward sweep has been completed.

STOPPING

The best way to put on the brakes is with 'braking strokes', which are short and quick alternating back strokes. By sitting up straight and planting your braking strokes firmly in the water at your hip, you should be able to stop your kayak with three quick powerful strokes.

Three quick braking strokes should stop your kayak at any time.

DRAW STROKE

Draw strokes are used to move your kayak sideways and are handy for pulling up beside somebody, or when approaching a dock.

There are two basic draws that we're going to look at: the T-stroke and the sculling draw.

T-STROKE

The T-stroke is the most basic draw stroke. It involves reaching out to the side of your kayak at around your hip, planting your blade, and then pulling yourself and your boat sideways. For the most effective stroke, rotate your torso aggressively to the side that you're performing the stroke on, get your paddle shaft as vertical as possible,

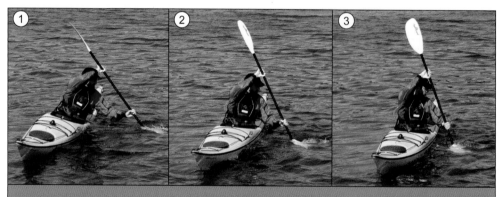

The T-stroke is planted with head and upper body turned towards. The top hand stays relatively fixed while the lower hand pulls towards the hip.

Before the stroke hits the kayak, curl your wrists forward to turn your blade 90-degrees and slice it back out for another draw stroke.

and fully submerge the blade before pulling on it. To get your paddle shaft vertical you'll need to reach across your upper body with your top hand. This takes some real balance, so you might want to start by practicing your draw stroke with your top hand lower, and in front of your face. With your blade planted firmly in the water, pull your lower hand in toward your hip. Your top hand will stay stationary, acting as the pivot point for the stroke.

When pulling the paddle to your hip, it's important that you stop its progress before the paddle contacts your kayak, where it can get pinned and pull you off balance. Although you have the option of simply pulling your paddle blade up and out of the water, the T-stroke involves a more elegant in-water recovery. The idea is to get your blade back to its starting point while keeping it in the water. To do this, you'll curl your wrists forward to turn your blade 90-degrees so that you can effortlessly slice it back out to the side of your kayak.

As you go through these motions, fight the urge to tilt your kayak into the draw stroke and keep your boat flat on the water instead. This allows water to flow under your kayak and prevents it from piling up on the side. The most efficient draw actually involves tilting your kayak away from the stroke. This is something to strive for, although it requires a high level of balance and is a technique that will take time to perfect.

If you find that your boat is turning when you use the draw stroke, it means that you're pulling your draw too far forward or too far back. If your draw is too far forward, you'll pull your bow towards your paddle. If your draw is too far back, you'll pull your stern towards your paddle.

Not only is the in-water recovery of the T-stroke elegant and efficient, but it will improve your paddle dexterity and will get you started on feathering your blade in the water. This is a key skill that will lead to a heightened awareness of both how to support yourself in the water, and how to 'slip', or minimize, resistance.

SCULLING DRAW

The sculling draw is a much more powerful draw than the T-stroke, but it requires significantly more paddle dexterity—which is why it's a great stroke to learn!

The sculling draw is set up in the same way as the T-stroke—with your upper body rotated towards it, your paddle shaft positioned as vertically as possible, and your blade fully planted in the water at 90 degrees from your hip. The difference between the two strokes lies in how you'll pull on your paddle. Instead of pulling your blade directly into your hip, you'll use something called a sculling motion. This sculling motion lets you pull steadily on your paddle, and bypasses the recovery phase that the T-stroke requires.

The key to sculling is keeping your paddle blade moving along a short path forward

Sculling involves moving your paddle blade along a short path alongside your kayak with the power face open to the oncoming water.

With your hands held in relatively fixed positions, you will need to use your torso rotation to provide much of the power for the stroke.

and backward about a foot or two out to the side of your kayak, with a blade angle that opens your power face to the oncoming water and pulls your paddle away from your kayak. This unique blade angle is commonly referred to as a 'climbing angle'. Climbing angle means that the leading edge of your paddle blade is higher than the trailing edge. It's the same as spreading jam on toast: picture the knife's angle as it glides over the bread's surface, leading edge higher than the trailing edge. To maintain a climbing angle on your blade while performing the sculling draw you'll cock your wrists slightly back as you slice your blade forward. You'll then make a quick transition and curl your wrists slightly forward as you slice your blade backward. Keep in mind that the change in blade angle is subtle. If you open your power face too much, you'll be pushing your kayak forward and backward rather than drawing it sideways.

Using this sculling technique, you can apply steady drawing pressure with your paddle blade and move your boat laterally at a surprising speed. Don't forget that just like any other stroke, the power for your sculling draw comes from your torso rotation. This is why it's so important that you turn your body aggressively into the stroke. The forward and backward movement of your paddle can then be driven by your torso rotation, while your arms will stay in a relatively fixed position.

STERN RUDDER

Stern rudders are the most powerful way to control your kayak when moving forward, and the best way to control a boat when surfing waves. There are two forms of the stern rudder: the stern pry, and the stern draw. Both strokes start from the same position—with your paddle planted firmly in the water behind your body and parallel to your kayak. To do this, and still keep your hands in front of your body in the power position (Golden Rule #2), you'll need to use some aggressive torso rotation (Golden Rule #3), which means turning your whole upper body towards your rudder. Your front hand should be held comfortably in front of your chest. From this position you can either push away with the backside of your paddle blade, which is called the stern pry, or you can draw water towards your stern with its power face, which is called the stern draw. The stern pry is by far the more powerful of the two strokes and the most commonly used.

The stern pry involves pushing away with the backside of your paddle and is the most powerful way to control your kayak when moving forward.

BOW DRAW

The bow draw is a great technique for quickly changing direction when moving forward. It involves planting your paddle, about a foot out to the side of your foot, with your blade angled so that your power face catches water. You can also tilt your boat away from your draw to help get your boat turning.

This stroke can generate a lot of force and so it's important to rotate your torso to the side where you're performing the stroke. This will protect your shoulders by keeping your arms in close to the body, and in the power position. Because you're catching water with this stroke, it will slow your boat down. As your kayak slows, draw the blade in to your toes to finish the stroke. You'll then be in a perfect position for a forward stroke to get yourself going again.

There isn't much support generated by the bow draw, because your paddle isn't in a good bracing position. You probably won't feel very comfortable with it when starting out, but as you gain confidence and balance, you will find the bow draw more helpful. The great thing about this stroke is that it lets you make powerful and precise corrections to your course, while keeping your forward paddling rhythm going.

The bow draw lets you make powerful and precise corrections to your course.

Initiate your turn with a forward sweep before planting your low brace.

Your paddle provides bracing support first – turning power second.

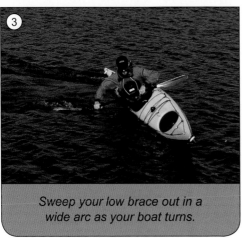

Sweep your low brace out in a wide arc as your boat turns.

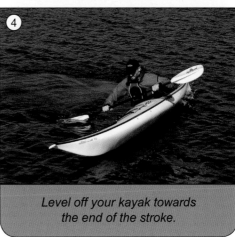

Level off your kayak towards the end of the stroke.

LOW BRACE LEAN TURN

The low brace lean turn is the most basic and fundamental of moving turns—and it's a skill that you will use in all types of water conditions. It combines the motions of a reverse sweep with the support of a low brace to make a smooth and effective turn. It should be noted that it will seriously slow your forward speed, often stopping you altogether.

The low brace lean turn starts with forward speed and is initiated with a forward sweep stroke on the opposite side to the lean turn itself. This means that if you want to turn to the right, you'll initiate the move with a forward sweep stroke on the left. With the turn initiated, you'll then rotate your upper body as if to take a reverse sweep on your right, and tilt your boat into this same direction. Unlike the reverse sweep that is used when the kayak is sitting flat on the water, the primary focus of your paddle is now to provide bracing support, while its secondary purpose is to provide turning power. This means that your blade will be almost flat to the water surface, although it will need a slight climbing angle so that it stays on the surface without diving, and can be used to help turn your boat. (Climbing angle is described earlier, in the section on the 'Sculling Draw'.)

As your boat begins to turn, hang on to your low brace and slowly sweep your bracing 'reverse sweep' forward while keeping your boat on edge. As your boat reaches the end of its turn, your blade should have swept forward to a point directly out to the side from your hip.

As your kayak slows down, the amount of support you'll get from your brace drops considerably. This means that you'll need to flatten out the tilt on your kayak towards the end of the turn, before you've scrubbed all your forward speed, and you lose the support from the brace.

HIGH BRACE LEAN TURN

The high brace lean turn is virtually the same as the low brace lean turn, only you'll be using a high brace for support on the inside of the turn, and you won't need to use the same reverse sweep motions. Instead, you'll plant your high brace out to the side of your kayak, just behind your hip, and with a climbing angle on the blade. This climbing angle will allow you to get steady support from your blade and help turn your kayak as your boat travels forward.

Start with some forward speed, and then initiate your turn with a forward sweep stroke on the opposite side to your turn. You'll then tilt your kayak in the direction of your turn and place your high brace on that same side. You'll need to cock your wrists back to establish a climbing angle on your blade. In order to keep your shoulders safe through the high brace turn, keep your arms in relatively close to your body and your top hand low—in what we like to call the 'nose pick' position.

As a final note, remember that the support you get from your brace comes from its motion relative to the water. This means that as you slow down through the turn, you'll get less support from the brace and will need to level off your kayak.

1

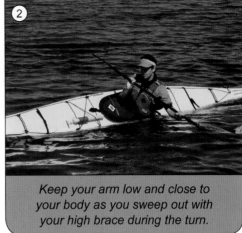

2

After initiating the turn, plant your high brace with a climbing angle.

Keep your arm low and close to your body as you sweep out with your high brace during the turn.

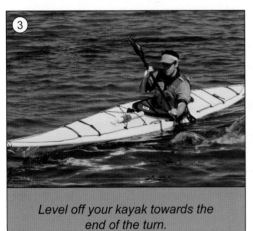

3

4

Level off your kayak towards the end of the turn.

The high brace lean turn leaves you in great position for a powerful forward stroke.

CHAPTER FIVE

SWIMMING • ASSISTED RESCUES• SELF RESCUES

Although the title of this chapter might imply that we'd be looking at specialized skills designed exclusively to save lives, the reality is a little less dramatic. The following rescue techniques are simply fundamental skills that you need to have to deal with that inevitable unplanned swim out of a kayak, the one that is in so many of our futures. For many paddlers, the thought of a capsize is stomach-churning, and the resulting swim is considered to be the absolute "worst case scenario"—all of which makes this an even more important topic to cover in this book. By learning and practicing these rescue skills, you'll boost your confidence and comfort level on the water, which in turn will allow you to progress as a kayaker.

The rescue techniques presented here are indeed designed to deal with potentially life-threatening situations. As should be clear by now, when paddling on the ocean (especially in exposed areas), there are more hazards to contend with than inland on flat water, and more opportunities for very serious situations to present themselves. So, if you plan on paddling on open seas, it's essential that you arm yourself with these fundamental skills, and that you practice them in a controlled environment so that you can perform them with confidence under duress.

Whatever type of rescue situation that you find yourself dealing with, the most important goal of any rescue must be—above all else—to get everyone involved to a place of safety. While some approaches might look smoother or more polished than others, you must never lose sight of this goal. In rescues, we like to say that 'there are no points for style'. In other words, the acid test for any rescue technique is whether it works quickly, safely, and consistently in real-world scenarios. If it does, then it's a good rescue technique. However, some rescue techniques simply do work better than others, and so we're going to focus on the techniques that have stood the test of time.

It's important to note that all the rescue techniques demonstrated in this book assume the use of a kayak with fore and aft bulkheads, and waterproof hatches, which will keep the ends of the kayak from filling with water when it's upside down. Without these safety features, the entire interior volume of your kayak can fill with water, sinking it to the bottom before a rescue can be performed. In the absence of bulkheads, air bags in the ends of the boat can be used for flotation, but they must be very securely anchored inside. If your kayak doesn't have lots of flotation in both the bow and stern, get one that does!

SWIMMING

Swimming is the simplest form of self-rescue, and sometimes it may be the best strategy. It also might be your only choice if you're paddling alone or with a group that isn't familiar with capsize recovery techniques. If you think that swimming is your only option, then it is only prudent that you always remain within a comfortable swimming range from shore. This means that if you're paddling on a lake, you'll have to always stick to an accessible shoreline instead of crossing the center of the lake.

If you are attempting to swim with your boat, flip your kayak back upright so that it glides across the water more easily. In sheltered conditions you can try pushing it ahead of you and then swim to catch up to it; otherwise tow it behind you. Slide your paddle into the cockpit or under a deck bungee to make swimming easier. You can also use your paddle to help propel yourself with powerful back strokes.

Something to keep in mind is that if wind and waves are present, swimming all your gear into shore might be very difficult or downright impossible, and your gear may quickly become irretrievably scattered. Of course, on the open seas, losing your boat and paddle is nothing short of disastrous. This is why you must be well versed at practical rescue techniques before entering that demanding environment.

ASSISTED RESCUES

An assisted rescue is a team effort. Although the rescuer is in charge of the proceedings, the fastest and most effective assisted rescues also require the active participation of the swimmer as well.

There are generally three parts to most rescues:

- The capsized kayak is returned to an upright position.
- The swimmer re-enters their boat and re-establishes control.
- The water is removed from the kayak.

There is no rigorous order that these three parts must follow. In fact, we'll see that the sequence in which they should be accomplished changes depending on the specific rescue technique. What is important is achieving the goal of getting a swimmer back in their seat, in control of their emptied boat.

The rescuer lifts as the swimmer pushes down on the stern to pop the cockpit out of the water and drain it.

The rescuer then rotates the empty kayak upright, being careful not to scoop any water into the cockpit.

With the boat empty, both parties can prepare for a re-entry.

ASSISTED BOW TIP OUT

The assisted bow tip out is a fast and highly dependable rescue technique. It's particularly effective because it gets an overturned and swamped kayak upright while simultaneously draining most of the water from the boat. This allows the swimmer to re-enter a virtually dry kayak, saving a huge amount of time that would otherwise be spent pumping the boat out, and greatly decreasing the time that the swimmer is exposed to cold water.

To perform an assisted bow tip out, the rescuer should approach the bow of the capsized kayak, remaining perpendicular to it so that the two boats create a rough 'T' formation. The swimmer then goes to the stern of the capsized kayak, and presses down on the stern while the rescuer lifts the bow upward and hauls the bow across the spray deck. Elevating the bow breaks the seal created by the cockpit against the water and causes the water inside the boat to flow down to the stern bulkhead and drain out. When the water is drained out of the cockpit, the rescuer then rotates the empty kayak upright, and the swimmer can prepare to re-enter.

One of the challenges during this kind of rescue is managing the paddles. Secure both the swimmer's paddle and your paddle by either holding them in your lap, or sliding them under a deck bungee.

RE-ENTRIES

There are many ways to re-enter a kayak from the water, but some techniques are definitely easier and faster than others.

The job of the rescuer is to stabilize the swimmer's kayak during the re-entry process. The best way of doing this is to position the kayaks side by side, and then to commit your body weight onto the empty boat with a firm grip on the perimeter lines. This stabilizing technique is amazingly effective and is not solely limited to rescue situations. It can be used whenever another kayaker can benefit from rock-solid stability, such as when someone wants to shed a layer on the water, or needs to adjust his or her foot pedals. It's also the best way to stabilize a kayak for someone who is getting in or out at a dock.

Side Sit Re-entry

The side sit re-entry is the quickest way to get back into your boat from the water, but it requires a fair amount of strength and dexterity.

As the swimmer, approach your kayak from the outside (opposite to the stabilized side), just behind the cockpit. Grab the cockpit rim and let your legs float to the surface behind you. With a powerful kick of your legs and a simultaneous strong pull of your arms, heave your chest up on top of your kayak's stern deck. With your head facing the stern, lift your legs into the cockpit and slide into the kayak, twisting into your normal sitting position. Strive to stay as low as possible throughout this maneuver for maximum stability.

The side sit re-entry is the quickest way to get back into your boat from the water.

Wriggling into the kayak during a face up re-entry.

Face Up Re-entry

The face up re-entry doesn't require as much explosive power as the side sit re-entry, and can be a better choice for swimmers who find the side sit challenging.

As the swimmer, position yourself at the stern end of your kayak, between your boat and the rescuer's. Throw an arm over the end of each boat, and then hook one leg up and into your boat's cockpit. Now swing your second leg up and in to the cockpit as well, and wiggle your way into the seat while keeping your weight as low to the kayak as possible.

Sling Re-entry

If neither the side sit nor the face up re-entry are working, a sling can come in handy. Slings are simply pieces of tubular webbing or rope that are tied in a long loop. When secured, a sling works just like a step, allowing you to get your chest up onto the stern of your kayak more easily, at which point you can then lift your legs into the cockpit and twist into the sitting position.

Scoop

If for some reason, none of the other re-entries are working, then the scoop might be the only option. The idea behind the scoop is to float the swimmer back into their kayak, allowing the rescuer to rotate the swamped boat and its occupant back upright.

As the rescuer, you'll hold the swamped boat on its side while the swimmer slides their legs as far as they can into the kayak (well past the pedals if possible). The swimmer will then lean all the way back onto their stern deck to lower their center of gravity as much as possible. The rescuer can then pull up hard on the cockpit coaming and right the swamped kayak. Although you can get a swimmer into their boat very quickly with the scoop, you're not really getting them out of the water as fast, because they'll still have a very full kayak to contend with, and it can take considerable time and effort to pump the boat out.

The scoop is an effective rescue for swimmers who are unable to lift themselves out of the water with their own power, whether due to exhaustion, injury, or a lack of upper body strength.

The scoop is a good re-entry if the swimmer is unable to lift themselves out of the water.

A hand held pump requires two hands to use and so it's nice to have someone stabilizing your kayak while doing so.

PUMPING WATER OUT OF A BOAT

After a swimmer re-enters their kayak, depending on the rescue technique, it may be necessary to pump water out of the cockpit compartment. As the rescuer, your job is only half finished when you've got the swimmer back into their kayak. It's important that you continue to stabilize their kayak until they have pumped all water out and have regained full control of their boat.

As discussed earlier in this book, there are a few different types of pumps, each with their own strengths and weaknesses. Regardless of what type of pump you have, you should know that it takes a surprisingly long time to pump water out of a kayak. If shore is close by, and a good landing site presents itself, it may be easiest to land and empty your boat on shore.

Something to consider is that if there are any waves to contend with while using a hand pump, it will be best to get your spray skirt back on your boat before you start pumping, to prevent more water from splashing in. You can then slide the pump down the waist of your skirt, or through an upturned corner along the side of the skirt.

SELF-RESCUES

If you choose to paddle alone, it's absolutely mandatory that you have a few bombproof self-rescue techniques to fall back on. In the absence of any truly dependable self-rescues, your only option is to limit yourself to paddling in very sheltered locations within easy swimming distance from shore. Self-rescue techniques are challenging and require a lot practice to perfect. Furthermore, while these techniques work very well in calm conditions, they are much more difficult to perform in wind and waves.

If you do take an unscheduled swim while paddling alone, your first priority should be to keep a hold of your equipment. With your boat and paddle in hand, there are a number of self-rescue options available to you.

SCRAMBLE

The scramble is just what it sounds like: a rescue technique in which you climb back on top of your boat and get back into the cockpit, all without the aid of another paddler's help, or the use of any other dedicated rescue gear. It's quite a balancing act!

From the water, flip your boat upright. If possible, try to lift the bow as high as arm's length as you flip it, because this will scoop the least amount of water into the cockpit. To re-enter, approach your boat from the side, at the stern. While keeping a hold of your paddle, secure a good grip on the back of the coaming with one hand and reach across to the other side of the boat with the other. Now pull yourself up, keeping

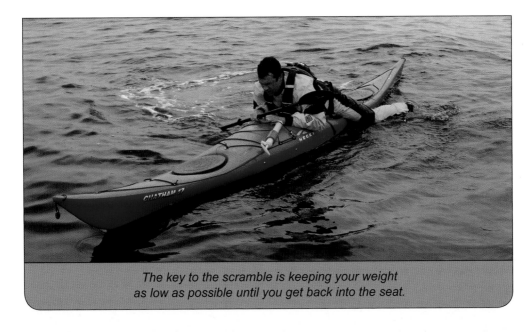

The key to the scramble is keeping your weight
as low as possible until you get back into the seat.

After pulling your chest on top of your kayak, you can hook a foot over the paddle shaft for support.

Stay low and keep your weight on the paddle float side of the kayak as you twist back into the seat.

Keeping your paddle perpendicular to the kayak ensures that the paddle float is providing maximum support.

your chest down, onto the stern deck. Staying as low as possible, throw a leg over the kayak so that you're straddling it with your head towards the bow. You can stabilize yourself by trailing a leg in the water either side of the boat and continuing keep your weight as low as you can. Now work your way forward and drop your butt down into the seat. Use your paddle for support as you pull your legs in under the deck. To get more support from your paddle, consider attaching a paddle float to a blade before starting your scramble.

PADDLE FLOAT RESCUE

The paddle float rescue uses your paddle as an outrigger, with a float attached to one blade to create a buoyant support.

To perform a paddle float self-rescue, securely attach the float to one end of your paddle. If you're using a paddle float that requires inflating, you'll need to blow it up after it is attached to your paddle. Flip your kayak upright, and then place the paddle across the back of the cockpit coaming, perpendicular to the kayak, with the paddle float in the water as far out to the side as possible. Most kayaks have bungees directly behind the cockpit that are designed to anchor a paddle in place for this very purpose. Holding the paddle and the coaming of the cockpit in one hand and reaching across to grab the coaming with the other hand, you're ready to pull yourself up and onto your kayak.

To get up on your kayak, let your feet float to the surface behind you, then kick hard and pull your chest up onto the boat. You can then hook a foot over your paddle shaft to get additional support while you turn towards your stern, and maneuver your other leg into the cockpit. Make sure that you continue to hold your paddle perpendicular to the kayak throughout the rescue. Keep your center of gravity low and your weight on the paddle float side of the kayak. Hook your second leg into the cockpit and, keeping your weight on the paddle float side of your kayak, twist your body back into the seat.

Once you're back in the driver's seat, you can bring your paddle in front of you and continue to use the float for support, while you pump out any water in the cockpit.

CHAPTER SIX

TRAVELING ON THE WATER

PADDLING IN A GROUP • WEATHER • PADDLING IN WIND
UNDERSTANDING TIDE AND TIDAL CURRENTS
PADDLING IN SURF • KAYAK TRIPPING

PADDLING IN A GROUP

Paddling with other folks is fun and it provides a great opportunity to learn new techniques and approaches. Even more importantly, paddling in a group is far safer than paddling alone, although there are a few ground rules that must be established.

When you decide to paddle as part of a group, you are becoming a member of a team (even if the team consists of only two). As such, you need to work with your other team members to accomplish the intended mission as safely and as enjoyably as possible. If you're just paddling a short distance in sheltered waters with a couple of buddies, this isn't such a big deal. For extended trips on the open ocean, especially

if you're in a large group, or paddling with people who aren't close friends or family, the job of maintaining a solid and constructive group dynamic requires more careful consideration, attentiveness, and hard work.

When paddling in a group, it's important to realize that your goals or objectives may be very different from the others in your group. While you might be looking to burn off some steam over a long workout paddle, someone else may be interested in simply getting some fresh air. For this reason, it's important that the goals for an outing are established in advance so that each person knows what they are signing up for. It's also important that you be patient and accommodating, because even people with similar goals can have different and equally valid ways of reaching them. Whatever your goals, and however you decide to reach them, remember that your group is only as strong as the weakest paddler and that all members of the group are equally entitled to feeling safe and having fun while afloat.

PADDLE AND WHISTLE SIGNALS

Paddle signals and whistles come in handy when a group is spread out, or when conditions, like wind, prevent your voice from carrying over any real distance. Of course, any signals are only useful if everyone in your group knows how to interpret them, so go over the signals as a group before heading out.

Whistles do a great job of getting people's attention. It's universally accepted that a single whistle blast is used to simply draw attention, while three quick whistle blasts are used to indicate an emergency.

The paddle can also be used as a very simple means of communication when there is a large distance between paddlers, and hand signals won't be effective. You can tell someone to stop by holding your paddle in the air horizontally. To tell someone to go ahead, hold your paddle vertically.

TOWING

Towing a kayak is the most effective way to transport another boat across the water, and is useful in a variety of situations, including when someone is injured, seasick, or simply tired and struggling to make headway in strong wind or current. However, it's important to understand that towing someone is very taxing and the decision to tow another kayak over a long distance should not be made lightly.

All towline systems must include a quick release buckle that allows the towing paddler to break free of the towline at a moment's notice in case of emergency. In some conditions, such as surf or strong currents, towline entanglement presents a serious hazard, so exercise caution when towing.

For the in-line tow, a longer towline is preferable and safer for long distances.

In-line Tow

The in-line tow is the most basic towing setup and simply involves clipping the tow boat onto the bow of the boat to be towed. For the smoothest ride, choose a towline with some stretch (many towlines have a built-in section of shock cord), to lessen the jerking of the line behind you. Short towlines, also called cow tails, are really quick to deploy and work well for short distance towing. For longer distances, a longer towline is preferable and safer because it will minimize the chances of a collision between the two boats.

Contact Tow

A contact tow is a good, fast towing technique for short distances. To perform a contact tow, position yourself alongside the other paddler's kayak, with the boats hard together. It doesn't matter if the person to be towed is in front of you, or behind. Have the other paddler grab a hold of your perimeter lines and lean aggressively onto your

A contact tow is a good, fast towing technique for short distances.

boat for stability. You can now paddle the two rafted boats as one. You may find that it helps to shift your grip on your paddle towards one end of the shaft in order to reach the water over the kayak being towed.

The beauty of this tow is the speed at which you can start towing, and the fact that you don't need any specialized equipment to do it.

Towing a Swimmer

If you find yourself having to tow a swimmer, the piggy-back technique is the best method. The swimmer climbs up onto your stern deck, lies chest down, and secures a firm grip around the rescuer's waist or deck hardware. The lower the swimmer keeps their center of gravity, the more stable the kayak will be.

This technique works well because it keeps the swimmer's core out of the water. Not only does this keep the swimmer warmer, it also reduces drag, making towing easier.

*The piggy-back technique keeps the swimmer out of the water,
which keeps them warmer and reduces drag.*

WEATHER

Weather is always a major concern for kayakers, especially for paddlers on the open ocean. Weather can blow in quickly and bring rain, wind, lightning, and fog—all of which can wreak havoc on a kayaker's carefully laid plans.

Of course, you'll always check the weather forecast before heading out on the water. If you're on a multi-day trip, you can get the latest marine forecast information on a handheld VHF radio. When considering weather conditions relative to paddling hazards, rain typically isn't a problem. In fact, paddling in the rain can be really interesting. While visibility may be somewhat hindered, if the conditions are otherwise calm, and you choose a conservative route, there's no reason for rain to keep you off the water. The conditions that truly impact a paddler are wind, storms, and fog.

Storms can blow up surprisingly quickly, and on the water is an inhospitable and dangerous place to be during those times. Powerful winds can make forward progress impossible, and may even sweep kayaks far off course or out to sea. As winds build in intensity, paddling conditions will invariably deteriorate, and the water will get rougher as waves begin to form and break. Lightning also deserves the utmost respect. If a storm is beginning to build, be conservative—get off the water as soon as possible and wait for it to blow through.

Fog can also be a real hazard, especially in coastal areas where it is common and thick. Fog will of course reduce your visibility (sometimes to zero), but if it's thick enough it will also play tricks on your hearing, which can make dealing with other marine traffic very dangerous. If you plan on doing any paddling in fog, stick very close to the shoreline and avoid open water.

More than any other factor, we kayakers are ruled by wind and its effect on the water. A disregard for wind speed, its direction, or the prevailing wind patterns in a particular area, is a recipe for disaster. The next chapter offers some tips on how to deal with windy conditions.

When paddling in fog, stick very close to shore and avoid open water.

PADDLING IN WIND

Windy conditions should give even the best paddlers pause for thought. Wind can slow your progress down dramatically, and even prevent forward movement. Wind will also affect the surface of the water, making conditions much rougher. Some areas are notorious for funneling winds, so it's important to do your research and make special note of areas where this pattern occurs.

Paddling into a light to moderate headwind is just plain hard work, and if the wind is strong enough, it just isn't worth the effort. A relentless headwind will slow your progress to a desperate crawl or even stop it dead. While a head wind generally isn't that difficult to handle in terms of throwing you off balance, the bigger challenge comes from the mental toughness needed to work so hard for so little gain. Paddling into a heavy headwind is often fruitless and sometimes best abandoned. You may want to head to shore to wait out the wind, or you may need to take the long way around, using land features to protect yourself from the wind. You may also have the option

Land features can provide great protection from strong winds and because of this, a longer, protected route can often be the fastest and easiest route.

to turn and travel with the wind to an alternate landing-site. While this last strategy might leave you with the need to hitch a ride back to your vehicle, or even walk a fair distance, it's often a pretty good option.

Paddling with the wind is quite a different story. A tail wind will give you a helping push on your way, allowing you to cover more distance with less effort. Wind at your back may also generate 'following seas', where wind swell and waves are traveling in the same direction as the wind. These waves will often provide an additional boost of speed. Of course, these wind waves can quickly grow to a point where they become a major hazard for less experienced kayakers. The rise and fall of a kayak in following seas also has the ability to make people motion-sick, sometimes explosively so. The only solution for a sick paddler is to get off the water.

The trickiest wind conditions are when the wind is blowing from the side. You'll usually have to contend with waves coming at you on an angle, and your kayak will want to turn into the wind rather than keeping its course. The kayak's tendency to turn into the wind is called 'weather cocking'. A side wind is when a rudder or skeg is most useful (as discussed in the 'Using Rudders and Skegs' section).You can also edge your boat slightly to counteract the effects of wind, although this is tiring over extended periods of time. You may find that you simply need to paddle harder on one side of your kayak to keep your boat going straight.

If you have waves as well as wind coming in from the side, keeping your course becomes even more difficult, and breaking waves can threaten your stability. If the waves are big enough, tilt your boat into them and brace at the same time, while staying loose in the hips.

UNDERSTANDING TIDES & TIDAL CURRENTS

If you plan on doing any paddling on the ocean, you need to have an understanding of tides and tidal currents, and how they can impact your paddling.

The first thing to understand is the difference between tides and tidal currents. Tides are the movement of water up and down on a vertical plane. Currents are the movements of water back and forth on a horizontal plane. Tides and tidal currents mostly result from the gravitational effects of the moon, (and to a lesser degree, of the sun and planets) on the earth's seas and oceans. All bodies of water are subject to the gravitational pull of the moon and have tides, but on smaller bodies of water like lakes, the effect is too small to be noticed. The larger the body of water, the more pronounced the effect.

TIDES

Flood tides are when the water is rising; ebb tides are when the water is dropping. The high tide is when the water is at its highest, and the low tide is when the water is at its lowest. Because there are roughly 6.5 hours between these two times, there are two sets of tides each day, and the pattern repeats itself approximately every 24 hours. The whole tidal pattern itself changes with the phases of the moon, synchronized with the 28-day lunar cycle.

Because tides refer to the movement of water on a vertical plane, tidal information relates primarily to water depth (relative to a specific time) and to how high the water will creep up the shore. Since tides can vary greatly, they have a big impact on the accessibility of certain areas. It is not uncommon for channels with plenty of water at high tide to be completely dry at low tide.

TIDAL CURRENTS

Although in some areas tides can have a dramatic effect on water levels, tidal currents have a greater impact on sea kayakers. Tidal currents are caused by the massive amount of water that is forced around islands and up channels with the changing tides. When

Tidal currents can dramatically help or hurt your paddling progress and should dictate the route that you choose.

this water gets pushed through constricted channels, strong currents, and in some cases large rapids with towering waves and whirlpools are the result. For any tidal flow, there is a time of maximum flood, when water is flooding in at its greatest speed, and maximum ebb, when water is flowing back out at its highest speed. 'Slack tide' refers to the time when the water is between the flood and ebb, and at its calmest. A paddler can choose to travel at slack for minimal conditions, or use the flow of water during floods or ebbs to get a helping push in one direction.

While tides and tidal currents are implicitly linked, the two are NOT one and the same. Because the timing and height of tides provides little or no useful correlation to the direction and speed of tidal currents, tides and tidal currents should be considered totally separately for the purpose of navigation. Happily, both tides and tidal currents can be predicted with good accuracy using a tide and current atlas and appropriate marine charts. Tide and current atlases are different and updated each calendar year, so make sure you have a recent and relevant copy.

PADDLING IN SURF

In some coastal areas, you'll have little choice but to launch and land your kayak in a surf zone. Breaking surf represents one of the greatest challenges to any paddler. It's an incredibly dynamic and powerful environment that offers both amazing play possibilities, and potentially devastating beat-downs. In fact, there are books and DVDs dedicated solely to the topic, just because there is so much to learn about it. In this segment, we're going to limit our focus to the basics of how to safely launch and land in surf zones, and we'll assume that the conditions are mellow. If you find that you enjoy playing in the surf zone and want to expand your skill set, I strongly encourage you to seek out formal instruction from an established kayak club or paddling school.

CHOOSING A BEACH

Different beaches create different surf environments. On a beach with a long gradual slope into deeper water, waves will usually build more slowly and spill from the crest. These are the friendliest waves, and if the beach is sandy and the waves are small, it will be a great place to attempt landing and launching in surf.

A beach that drops off really quickly will cause waves to 'jack up' suddenly and collapse or 'dump' with tremendous force. There is incredible power in these waves, and this will not be a suitable beach for launching or landing a sea kayak.

Of course it's always preferable to land or surf at a sandy beach. A rocky shoreline strewn with big logs and other debris presents obvious hazards, and will make getting

A beach with a gradual slope usually offers waves that build and break more slowly. A steep sloped beach will have waves that build and dump very suddenly, which can be more hazardous for paddlers.

in and out a lot more difficult, and far more dangerous. If the waves just seem too big, or the conditions too gnarly, look for another launch site or bag the mission and try again later. Tides, wind and swell all have huge effects on surf, so a break is an ever-changing environment and a few hours can make a dramatic difference to the conditions.

LAUNCHING IN SURF

Launching in surf can be pretty tricky, but the good news is that launching is considerably easier than landing!

Start by taking the time to study the surf from shore. It is very common for a surf zone to have weak and strong break zones. Waves also come in sets, and it is important that you time your launch to coincide with the lull between sets. Once you decide to go for it, position your kayak at the edge of the water. Ideally, you'll be able to get into your boat on a sandy beach and get a buddy to push you in when the time is right. If this isn't an option, watch the rhythm of the incoming waves and jump into your boat between waves. Quickly get your skirt on and grab your paddle. The next wave should then push enough water up the beach to lift your kayak and let you pull away from shore.

When paddling out through surf, keep your boat perpendicular to the oncoming waves and paddle aggressively.

The initial entry from the beach is difficult, because it's often not deep enough to allow very powerful strokes. You may need to use your hands to 'scoot' into deeper water. The most important thing is to keep working forward with your boat perpendicular to the waves. Being perpendicular to the oncoming waves, your kayak will slice through them. Ideally you will pass over waves while they are green and unbroken, but this won't always be the case. When busting through a wave that is breaking, or on the verge of doing so, remember to lean forward and continue to paddle forward aggressively.

As a final tip, make sure that you're truly well past the breaking point of the waves before you relax. It's really easy to think that you're in the clear when really a set has just passed through. If you make this mistake, you'll find yourself right in the impact zone of the next big set.

LANDING IN SURF

Making a controlled landing in a surf zone is always challenging, and it requires both skill and timing to succeed. For this reason, if you are contemplating an attempt at a surf landing, you must also be prepared for the strong likelihood of a capsize.

If you get caught by a breaking wave, it will likely turn you sideways. In this case, tilt your boat slightly towards the wave and brace lightly against it.

Take your time to assess the conditions and to formulate a clear plan before committing to a landing. Ideally, you'll use the lull between sets to enter the surf zone. As you paddle towards the beach, you may need to back paddle or to put on the breaks to prevent a wave from picking you up and surfing you into shore. In a perfect world, you'll let waves roll by your kayak and chase them from behind. By chasing a wave all the way onto the beach, you'll have a moment to quickly pop your skirt, leap out of your kayak, and drag it clear before the next wave hits. Of course, this doesn't always work out so smoothly. If the next wave hits before you're ready, be mindful of your kayak because it can get tossed around. One of the most common surf injuries occurs in the shallows just off the beach, and results from boats being thrown into unsuspecting paddlers' legs. Always avoid being between a boat and the beach. If a kayak is fully loaded with gear, it is even more dangerous.

When traveling with a group, the best strategy is to have the two strongest paddlers be the first and last to land. The rest of the group should head in one at a time, waiting for the go ahead signal from shore before proceeding. Those on shore can help haul boats up the beach and stabilize kayaks as paddlers climb out. Just remember to never stand between a boat and the beach, or directly in front of an incoming kayak.

KAYAK TRIPPING

Kayak tripping can be one of the most invigorating, satisfying and even therapeutic activities, but if you don't adequately prepare yourself, it can end up being memorable for very different reasons.

CHOOSING A TRIP

When choosing a trip, know that there is no right or wrong decision. A paddling destination doesn't necessarily need to be remote or exotic, nor does it need to be challenging. The key to a successful trip is to choose a route and itinerary that will meet the goals and objectives of those who are involved. Alternatively, if you already have a specific trip in mind, it will be a case of finding the right combination of paddlers who will share your enthusiasm for the trip being planned, and have the right skill sets and equipment to complete it.

If you are choosing a group for a specific trip, there are a few factors that you'll need to consider. Your group size may be limited by park restrictions, environmental concerns, or the size of campsites. Some campsites, such as beaches that get routinely flooded, can sustain more traffic than fragile, dry environments where disruptions can kill fragile vegetation that requires decades to regenerate. Generally, twelve is considered a recommended maximum group size, although I prefer a group of three to six paddlers.

One of the first things you'll want to do when planning a trip is acquire maps or charts for the area, as well as a guide book if there's one available. There may be hazards to avoid, or some great sights that you won't want to miss. If your trip is coastal in nature, you'll also want to figure out what the tides and tidal currents will be doing—it might be necessary to paddle through some constricted channels subject to tidal flow, or avoid mud flats at low tide. With all this information, you can start to make an accurate trip plan.

One of the biggest remaining factors that will dictate your trip plan is the distance that can be traveled by your group each day. Most groups generally travel between two and four knots under ideal conditions. A group of relative beginners will cruise around two knots per hour, while a strong group will cruise closer to three knots. In ideal conditions, very fit paddlers who are consciously attempting to cover distance may average closer to four knots per hour. Of course, the wind, weather, and tidal currents can have something to say about this, which is why it is important to always have reasonable bail out and contingency plans.

BAIL-OUTS AND CONTINGENCIES

When planning any kayak trip, you'll want to make sure that you have plenty of camp and take-out options along the way and that you build in 'rest' or 'storm' days so that you won't feel the need to press on in poor conditions. Many of the worst and most dangerous decisions stem from the feeling that there is no option but to stick to the original plan.

PRE-TRIP SAFETY PLANNING

Before embarking on any trip, you should always create a float plan and file it with a friend who won't be on the trip. A float plan consists of a basic outline of your proposed route and the associated timeframe. It should include possible bail outs and contingency plans too. This float plan can dramatically speed up the time it takes for your group to be found if a rescue ever becomes necessary.

A float plan should be left before leaving on any trip.

KAYAK TRIPPING ETIQUETTE

One of the fundamental reasons that we kayak is to get outdoors and interact with the natural environment. When we're out there, we need to look upon ourselves as caretakers of this wonderful world. The motto 'Take only pictures and leave only footprints' is a worthy one, and a credo that is easy to adopt, especially since a sea kayak has more than enough room for you to pack everything out. And in some cases, this really does mean everything, right down to our own human waste!

Due to the very real threat of forest fires, campfires are not permitted in many areas, but if you are allowed to build one, keep your fires small and on the beach below the high tide mark. The sea can then wash your site clean.

When it comes to wildlife, keep in mind that we're trespassing on their territory. Feeding wild animals, even unintentionally, does them a grave disservice. Bears that become desensitized to humans and start associating them with an easy meal will likely become 'problem bears'—and often end up being destroyed.

GLOSSARY OF TERMS

Assisted rescue A rescue technique performed with the aid of at least one other person in addition to the swimmer

Back band Padded band of material that provides back support behind the seat of the kayak

Backrest Rigid seatback (often padded and adjustable in angle and height) that provides back support

Bilge Bottom of the inside of a boat

Bilge pump Device for pumping water out of a boat

Bow The front of a boat

Bowline Cord attached to the front of the boat - useful for towing or tying the boat to a dock

Bulkhead A waterproof wall that divides the interior of a kayak, creating flotation and storage areas

Bungee Shock-cords or bungee cords are the elastic lines on the deck of a kayak – perfect for securing gear within easy reach (water bottles, sunscreen, ball cap, etc.)

Capsize The overturning of a boat so that it goes from being right side up to upside down

Cargo The items transported in a boat

Chart A nautical chart is a marine map referencing water features, including depths, shorelines, scale, aids to navigation (like lights and buoys), and other features essential to marine navigation

Climbing angle The leading edge of your paddle blade is higher than the trailing edge

Coaming The lip around the cockpit that allows the attachment of a spray skirt

Cockpit The sitting area in a kayak

Compass A magnetic device that indicates magnetic north and the other corresponding points of direction over 360 degrees

Course The compass direction of travel to a destination

Deck The top of a kayak

Deck line Rope or shock-cord attached to a kayak's deck, used for securing items on deck or to make it easier to grab the boat

Drain plug A stopper, usually mounted in the stern, that can be removed to drain a kayak

Dry bag A waterproof bag with a seal (usually a roll-top closing system) that keeps water out

Ebb tide The outgoing tide and the resulting decrease in water depth; see 'Flood tide'

Eddy The quiet water behind an obstacle in current, where water flows back in the opposite direction to the main flow

Edging To tilt your kayak to one side

Feather The twist, offset, or difference in angles between the two blades of a kayak paddle

Float bags Air-tight bags that are secured inside a kayak to displace water and create flotation

Float plan An outline of the route and schedule of a kayak trip

Flood tide The incoming tide and the resulting increase in water depth; see 'Ebb tide'

Following seas When wind swell and waves travel in the same direction as the wind

GPS (Global Positioning Unit) A battery-powered electronic device that very accurately calculates positions and courses based on satellite information

Handles Carrying toggles found at the bow and stern of a kayak

Hatch The opening into a cargo compartment in a kayak

Hull The bottom of a boat

Kayak A watercraft propelled by a double-bladed paddle

Knot A measurement of speed – one nautical mile per hour

Life jacket A flotation device worn like a vest

Nautical mile Unit of distance used on the sea – approximately 1.87 kilometers or 1.15 'land' miles

Navigation The art and skill of determining your position, and selecting a safe route to your intended destination

Paddle Kayak paddles are double-bladed devices for propelling the boat; canoe paddles have only one blade

Paddle float A flotation device that attaches to one end of a paddle to create extra stability

Paddle leash Tether that attaches a paddle to a kayak

Perimeter lines Cords that run around the edges of the deck on a kayak, making the boat easier to grab

PFD Personal Flotation Device – see 'life jacket'

Portage To carry a kayak or canoe overland

Put-in The location where you start your trip

Re-entry Getting back into a kayak from the water

Rescue A process whereby people at risk are returned to a situation of safety

Ripcord The cord at the front of the spray skirt or spray deck that you pull to remove the skirt

Rip tide Strong current on a beach, created by waves – potentially very dangerous

Roof rack System of two bars that mount to the roof of a vehicle for transporting kayaks and other loads

Rudder Foot-controlled steering mechanism mounted at the back of a kayak

Scupper Hole that goes through a boat allowing water to drain off the deck back into the sea/lake/river

Sea state Surface conditions of the ocean resulting from winds, swell and currents

Self rescue A rescue technique where the swimmer re-enters their kayak without aid from a second party

Skeg A blade or fin that drops into the water to help a kayak go straight

Skirt See 'spray skirt'

Sling or stirrup A loop of webbing or rope used to aid a swimmer re-enter a kayak from the water

Spray skirt (also called 'spray deck') Nylon or neoprene skirt worn around the waist - attaches to the kayak coaming to keep water out of the boat

Stern Back of the boat

Swim Slang for capsizing and ending up in the water out of your boat

Takeout The location where your paddling trip ends

Thigh hook, or thigh brace The curved flange in a kayak's coaming that the leg braces against

Tidal rip Strong current created by changes in tide height

Tide and current tables (also called 'tide and current atlas') The collected calculations for tide and current information (times, heights, speeds); organized based on the calendar year, so a recent version is required for accurate information

Tie-down Strap or rope used to secure a kayak to the roof of a vehicle

Track 'Go straight'; used to describe a boat's ability to move in a straight line

VHF (Very High Frequency) Radio system commonly used in the marine environment; limited to a line-of-sight direct path between the transmitter and the receiver

Weather cocking The kayak's tendency to turn into the wind

Wind wave Waves formed by the effects of wind on the surface of water

Index

Outdoor Parents, Outdoor Kids
The Ultimate Guide
By Eugene Buchanan

Award-winning author Eugene Buchanan extends parents a helping hand in getting their kids outside and instilling in them a respect for their health and the environment.
$19.95 · 304 Pages

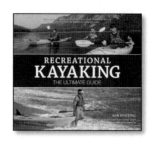

Recreational Kayakin
The Ultimate Guide
By Ken Whiting

This easy-to-read guide makes paddling fun and safe for both nev and experienced paddlers looking to broaden their horizons.
$19.95 · 192 Pages

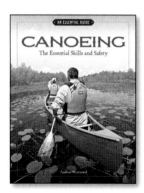

Canoeing
An Essential Guide
By Andrew Westwood

This guide provides beginner and experienced canoeists with the knowledge and skills necessary to safely and comfortably enjoy canoeing.
$19.95 · 144 Pages

Sea Kayaking Rough Waters
By Alex Matthews

Whether your interest is in paddlir in more challenging conditions, or learning new skills and concepts tł will boost your confidence for mo; sheltered paddling, this book is the one for you.
$19.95 · 128 Pages